*Lauren,*

# SELFISH

*You're already accomplished and triumped over so much!*

*My prayer is that my story fuels you for your next victory and empowers you to continue to live fully (and) enjoy the balance of your days.*

*Love,*

# SELFISH

Permission to Pause, Live, Love, and
Laugh Your Way to Joy

NAKETA REN THIGPEN

ThigPro Publishing
2020

ISBN 13: 978-1-7329838-7-8 (E-book)

ISBN 13: 978-1-7329838-0-9 (Paperback)

ISBN 13: 978-1-7329838-1-6 (Hardcover)

Library of Congress Control Number: 2018913229

Front Cover Image by Kardin K. Thigpen

Book design by Kardin K. Thigpen

Description: First Edition. | Pennsylvania: ThigPro, 2020

Published in the United States by ThigPro, an imprint of Thigpen's Professionals, LLC, Pennsylvania.

Manufactured in the United States of America

Send Copyright permission request to admin@thigpro.com

www.thigpro.com

To my loves Chief, Mally, Dupe, G-bunny's
Snow Pea, and our little Red King.

My reason for choosing to wake up, fuel up, and
replenish every day is to have more than enough life, love,
laughter, and joy to pour into you before and beyond the
grave, through eternity. God willing.

If we truly aspire to be selfless beings, we must carve out time to become intentionally selfish and take care of ourselves first. Only then can we ensure that we are truly giving of strength, energy, and time with full presence and without regret.

-Naketa Ren Thigpen

# CONTENTS

# SELFISH

# ACKNOWLEDGMENTS

As for me and my house....it is undoubtedly God first, and it is he, *El Roi*, whom I must thank and give the highest praise and glory to. The beginning, middle, nor end of this book would have occurred had it not been for his love and favor in my life!

My husband, Dean- my Chief, best friend, lover, and protector. I can't thank you enough for growing with me and loving on me when I wasn't the least bit malleable, patient, nor sweet. You are my heart's desire, my soul's half, only under God, and I will continue to love you toward your destiny.

Qamal, my handsome, creative, and visually pronounced son, I'm so amazed at how God uses you to help me gain perspective and deepen the depths of my joy. Although it isn't always clear to you, trust that God is strengthening you to make an imprint on this world so deep no man or woman can erase it. Qamal, you are destined for greatness...the world has no idea what's coming baby!

Messiah, my beautiful, talented, and incredibly fashion forward daughter, you are amazing. I am impressed with your tenacity and how God has his hand over your life. I pray that you always keep it there and stay under his covering while he grooms you to walk in the will of God towards your purpose....lights camera action Dupe!

Thank you to my parents, Robin Webster, Gary Webster, Kimberly Webster-Brinkley, Viola & Craig Thigpen, Sharon & Terrence Gilmore, for providing all that you have. Although you each entered and exited at different points in my life, I understand my "go through" and how it was necessary to "get to" the many levels in my life.

My birth parents, Robin and Gary, your life was undoubtedly traumatic and filled with hurdles I wouldn't dare to imagine. As a child, I saw and thought like a child and didn't understand nor care to. As an adult, I see beyond the surface and into the pain that you bore. Choosing to guide and love me was impossible when you couldn't love yourselves. I forgive you. I acknowledge the tough and beautiful choice you both agreed to when you move forward with bringing me into this world. For that, I am eternally grateful.

Mom-Kim, I appreciate you and the expansive love you've shown me before, during, and after divorcing my father. Always more than a stepmom, you have loved me since the moment you met my little ungrateful, bossy, back talking toddler self and embraced every ounce of change I've gown through with open arms and a non-judgmental heart. You have been an uncountable blessing for the Thigpen 4, and we love you to life. Qamal and Messiah love their *Nani*, Dean, and I love our Mom-Kim!

Mommy-Viola, my mother-in-love, you know God gave you to me at a very difficult time in my life, a time when I attempted to reflect a hard-shell, and you were able to see right through it...I'm so thankful for your strength and ability to pour into me. Who knew that I would fall head over heels in love with your son and claim your youngest child as my soul's other half. Well, maybe you did...

Craig, although you've been gone from this earth for more than eight years, I am thankful for your placement in my life- hard knocks and all! Rest in Peace.

Renee Lacey Tate, my maternal grandmother, guardian, and in loco parentis. Thank you for doing more than you had to. I wasn't always easy, and I could make things difficult. Though I'm sure you understand why I was so verbose and precocious, I realize that you were doing the best you could, given what you had. I've forgiven myself for my adolescent rebellion, and I've forgiven you for hurt and harm in my youth. I truly love you. Rest In Peace.

Aunt Carla & Uncle Clarence Cooper, my spiritual grounding began with you, and I will never forget where the sparks were first ignited. Thank you for taking me in, loving me, guiding me, chastising me with correction, keeping me safe, and letting me go into the world to make my own unavoidable (and sometimes avoidable) mistakes. You helped trained this former child in the way that I should go, and when I grew up, I did, in fact, return to the things of God that he foretold I would not depart from. Thank you from the depths of my soul and the breadth of my spirit. I love you.

Aunt Wanda Brown Jenkins, who departed the earth earlier than I wanted to let go, I couldn't have been made tougher if I was nurtured as a boxer. Hustle, drive, tenacity, perseverance, gumption...I credit them all to observing you. Like Aunt Carla, I thank you for taking me in on your turn, when it was simply God's will that I will be in your care and under your protection. I appreciate the hard lessons and the incredible boundaries that you made crystal clear. You and Aunt Carla are one of the biggest reasons I can stand in my No, unapologetically, and without regret. I thank you for that. I am grateful for that. I love you beyond time and gravitational barriers to that. Until we meet again, I will try not to deserve another beat down!

Aunt Terry & Uncle Tony Campbell, thank you for stepping in at moments when my parents weren't able. From the nursery through early elementary, you showed up when others couldn't, and I am grateful.

Momma Sherry and Pastor-Pop Terry Gilmore, you are the truest definition of the phrase Godparents. Although my birth parents did not know you to choose you when I was born, God appointed you to me, the honest honor I can receive, to have ordained angels over me in my early teen years and beyond. I thank you for your constant spiritual nurturing and growing with me as I develop my relationships, especially the one I have with God. More than a church family, *the absence of a blood tie is not a barrier between us. You've proven time and time again your love for me and everyone I'm connected to.* Eternally thankful for you in my life, my forever mi familia.

<u>My siblings and close cousins that had to deal with me along the way...</u>

Gary "Bg" Webster- Big Little Brother Bear (his sassy half Shalise, all their cubs, Brianna, Aniyah, Gary Jr. Gianna, and Jace Holton)

Frances Webster Brown- My Twin (her hilarious half Jeremy and resting angel Legend Lee)

Tanaya Webster- My original Chocolate Princess (and tiny but mighty little Queen Taylor Emani)

Robert Carter- Baby Brother (and littlest one's RJ and Ry'lee Naketa)

Sadira Thigpen & Tahjae Hilton- The best sister-in-law in the world and my favorite nephew

Junal Thigpen- My brother-in-law

Antoinette Campbell- My sister Cousin (and her little dancer Taraya)

Bryan Brown and Donald "Tre" Campbell- My brother-cousins (and their expanding clan)

Jules, Angie, and Nakia Anderson- My favorite South Philly Cousins!

Parental Guides and Mentors

Mrs. Karen Matthews

Dr. Anita Gordon Bell

Aunt Valerie Simmons

Aunt Joan & Uncle Joe Anderson

## My Beyond Blood Family

Shantel "Chi" Freeman & Corey Freemen; Godchildren: Amyle; Cherelle, Aulani, Kori Freeman

Vivian Green & My God-son Jordan Green

Kwame Holland

Ana & Carlos Guerrero (and littlest diva Alyssa)

Kurt and Bobbie Foedisch

Roxanne John Green & My Goddaughter Chozen Epiphany Green

# INTRODUCTION

I remember the way I exposed my mother's secret. It was intentional and liberating. For almost a year, I had lived through a state of fear. Something no eight-year-old should have to deal with. There is nothing unusual for a young child to dislike bedtime. For many children, it merely means that your fun runs through the house with Barbie doll-house role plays, and hopscotch time has come to an end. My nighttime anxiety was associated with the things that went bump in the night, had metallic smells, and was often accompanied by deep tone threats and pain, at least on a good night...

My grandmother's house, a small red brick, East Mt. Airy row home with dark panel walls, loop wool carpet woven in shades of brown, tan and black, and flat white ceilings was in retrospect, a mixed blessing. We were no longer on Elaine Street, in our small apartment just a few blocks away, where my mother was overwhelmed with bills and daily fights with my father. But, here I am, lying on top of a bunk bed that was technically too small for even my tiny frame, watching the orange and red light flicker up the side of the wall — listening to the hissing sound from the cigarette lighter, as if it hit the glass tube a little too hard each time. Here it comes, a nasty, yet old sugary sweet kind of sulfuric smell. I remember it like it was yesterday. I can still taste a bit of metallic taste on my tongue from the scent that burrowed through my nostrils as the smoke hits the air.

My mother would occasionally cough, breathing hard, then slowly. I'd hear her laugh a little to herself. At times, she would talk to herself. Most words were pretty unintelligible, especially to an eight-year-old. A little curse word here and there, a statement or two about a lost love or a failed workday. I lay there, trying to cover my nose so I wouldn't have to breathe in any more of that nasty sweet. I knew it was dangerous, I had a pretty good idea of what it was. But I didn't have any proof. I was afraid to peek down, so I'd lay there, silent. Trying to smother my coughs, pretending I didn't see, hear or smell her attempts to cover up her pain and heartache. I didn't know much about God at the time, outside of the fact that he would only choose 144,000 of us to save at the end of time. I wanted to be one of them, was hoping my mother would be too, so I prayed that whatever she lit, the fire would fizzle out before she drifted to sleep in an unproven drug haze, and we wouldn't all burn up in the middle of the dark and light of day. Compared to many others, if we made it through, this would be my version of a peaceful night.

There were other days, physically painful ones. As my anxious mind would tire out, and I'd get drowsy, no longer able to fight off the thoughts plagued with worry and fear, sometimes my step-grandfather would come in my room. Sometimes my mom wasn't home, working late, I guess. Other times she was passed out. He'd tap on the bunk bedpost and grip my shoulder to wake me up and pull me into his bedroom — so many thoughts walking down that very short but long hallway. I'd count the threads of snagged loops in the carpet, wishing I could shrink down into it and disappear. Maybe, I could get caught in one of the snags and never have to grow tall again, not even in the daylight... As we walked in the room and he'd shut the door behind us, switching the hooked latch below the faded gold knob, wondering why no one else could hear us, why no one would come to get me, why my mother wouldn't just wake up and save me from this torture.

Most nights, my grandmother was still at work. She worked most nights, graveyard shift at a nearby nursing home. On her days off, she slept downstairs on the living room couch. Some mornings when she returned home and came upstairs to get cleaned up and change from out of her nursing uniform, I was still lying in the front room, her bedroom, with her husband. Sometimes I would hear the opening of the door and then close it again. She'd go downstairs and go to sleep on the couch.

For all the years I lived in that house, I only remember her being upstairs in that bedroom once, and I don't even think it was for more than a few hours. There were so many intense moments. Our morning alarm clock was often the deafening sounds of yelling, screaming, pushing, and shoving in the kitchen, right below my bedroom. Reflecting the tension and intensity of our life were severely traumatic and constantly unnerving. But to us, it was normal. Get up, get washed, get dressed, and get out of the house. Simply walk up the street to school, place a smile on your face, and do your best in school. Oh, and try not to get into any fights that would force your step-grandfather to be called to the school, requiring you to come home early...

On the surface, I smiled like any other lower-middle-class kid. No one really questioned much, unless I had an explosive moment in school with a peer. Substitute teachers might assume I was a brat. As large as Mt. Airy was, the Cedarbrook section, where I spent the majority of my early years, was quite small. A few of the adults that worked in the school, including one of the crossing guards, lived on my block. They knew my family, some heard stories from our neighbors to the left or the right of our tightly built row home. Many saw the drunken rages my overly aggressive step-grandfather would have when he was pissed off at whatever irked him that side of the hour.

The full-time teachers in my elementary school were far from shocked when I was called to the principal's office for punching a boy in the throat that got too close during a game of freeze tag at recess. They were equally not surprised when I used inappropriate language to correct one of the fallacies of my peers when they'd say things, like, you can get pregnant from swallowing watermelon seeds. A pretty innocent assertion for kids whose parents refused to answer their questions about where babies come from. I, on the other hand, was ironically overly educated on the matter. My grandmother would enforce and reinforce the importance of me understanding biology and all of the scientifically correct names of our body parts. So as a natural giver, I'd share the knowledge with my peers. "What's that you say? A wee-wee? No, it's a penis, and you can only get pregnant if he ejaculates sperm into your vagina during sexual intercourse." I could be a slow learner, so it would take around 5 or 6 trips to the office before I could process why telling the truth about biology was such a bad thing in third grade.

Some of my offenses were intense, between the fighting and verbal infractions around biology, they'd feel forced to make the call home. When my step-grandfather would come up to the school, you could see the adults tense up with regret from making the call. You could also tell the moment the thought of, "Agh, I see why she's like that," would pour over their faces. Four out of five times, he was intoxicated to the hill, aggressive and verbally raw when he vomited his agitation through his one-way conversation. To put it mildly, he was verbally abusive to any female who crossed his path. Even though they had these moments of regret, understanding, and pity, no one ever intervened.

For my grandmother, it was pretty much understood and often noted how she felt. At least once a day, I'd hear the words, "Just don't embarrass me. What goes on in this house stays in this house... Don't make too much noise, don't bring too much attention. Be quiet." Don't get me wrong, she wasn't saying anything that my friends hadn't mentioned their parents or grandparents had said more than once in their house either. But for me, the messages were applied to more than just stomping up the steps or playing too loudly in the back yard with my cousins.

## The Early Scripts Show Up in Every Action We Take & Avoid

The scripts that are written in our youth matter more than we realize. So many of the moments that impacted my actions, taken and avoided, reflected what I learned before and during my time in that little row home in the Cedarbrook section of East Mt. Airy. One of the reasons I chartered a path as a Licensed Clinical Social Worker and felt pulled towards trauma-informed care to help victims become survivors' post-assault was because of the script I had and wanted to erase. I didn't want to be like the adults in my life when it came to protecting children. If I saw something, anything, I didn't want to huff and puff at the symptom and just be irritated at an inconvenient behavioral outburst that was clearly a cry for help. I wanted to be in a position to recognize and support them without having their life implode. Breaking free from the private expectation I set when I decided to eradicate that script would also become the fuel that propelled me beyond my clinical practice as a trauma specialist in pediatric and special delivery social work and into coaching and consulting as an entrepreneur many years later.

In my young adult years, those scripts would direct me towards serial monogamy with young men that resembled my inconsistent father and unbalanced friendships. It was inside the scenes of my subconscious attempts to play out this script that I'd learn to perfect my secret-keeping skills and nurturing others first as a proof of loyalty. Growing into my voice was difficult. Not because I was a shy, introverted kid. Far from it. I overcompensated to cover my pain. I can say emphatically that I was the most vocal in nearly any room, the first to jump in a fight if I saw someone being bullied, physically or verbally, and without hesitation at every age. I stood as a giver, finding new creative ways to show someone else how much they mattered to me, at times, even more than I mattered to myself. My outward resting face was always cheery, and I maintained a light disposition whenever I was in a public space.

The layer beneath my disposition had frayed edges, torn from unspoken trauma and confusion. Most people (adults and peers alike) would never access the deeper layers. Those who stepped over my undefined edge violated unspoken boundaries and took my kindness as a sign of gullibility and naivety. As a child, I felt the definition of my boundaries were implied in and through my actions. I felt very strongly that if I showed kindness, smiled, loved, and gave my loyalty, the same would be returned. As I grew stronger in my discernment, I'd learn that not everyone played with the same set of rules as I did, and I'd eventually learn to sharpen my "let go knife." Of course, this didn't come for some time, but when it did, I got quite good at cutting people from the ether of my life. Looking back, it would have served me well to discover and sharpen that ethereal weapon much earlier along my journey. But the reality is, everything was in its time, even if I couldn't see it.

For decades, I gave football stadium lengths of proverbial rope in all relationships, simply because I didn't want to waste energy on developing a new friendship. I had very few non-negotiables, and honestly, to this day, still do. Although my filter for letting people in is much more defined and my limits more clear, back then, when the early childhood scripts ruled my actions and inactions, as long as you didn't put your hands on me or someone I cared for or made me feel physically uncomfortable, I'd pretty much allow anything. Until my mature adult years, pre-therapy, I felt like those relationships at home, work, in my social circles, were healthy if they were absent physical or sexual abuse, and I was allowed to give others a safe space to share their secrets. It didn't really matter if that emotional safety was truly reciprocated, I needed to feel needed, and it gave me purpose. Those were my scripts. Everything outside of those things, were, well, normal....

## What to Expect from This Book

I wrote this book so that it would be a simple but not necessarily easy read. It's my life, complex and non-linear. My story of personal transformation as I grew from the thorns of trauma, loss, heartache, bad choices, and immeasurable mistakes that would snowball over multiple years. Nothing about writing this was easy for me, in fact,

I tried to write it on and off for almost eight years. At least I'd say I was writing it. The truth is, speaking about it is a whole hell of a lot easier because opening my mouth and sharing the most vulnerable parts of myself to help others not hide from themselves is my greatest gift. Writing sort of locks me into moments that I'd rather not relive. Especially, repeatedly through a grammatical editing process. I can admit, jotting notes in handwriting that only two people in the world can read and write in clear, concise sentences that people who don't know you can follow is a lot harder than most people realize. From here throughout the first four chapters, I gave myself and you, full *permission to slow down* and truly dive into the nitty gritty details of when my original early-year scripts were formulated, with the hope that you can see the parallels of your own.

So, in full vulnerability, and hopefully limited grammatical flubs, I share my story, altering a few names and setting details to respect the anonymity and privacy of the living and dead. My intention is not to blame or point fingers, I stand as a light, no longer afraid of the dark corners of my past, hoping that my truth with free at least one person reading this from the pain of theirs. We, especially as women, have been taught to nurture and care for everyone before ourselves. To play the background. Be incredibly good, but not too amazing. Speak up, but don't stand out. Feel free to say what's on your mind but be careful not to outshine the wrong person or embarrass anyone. Go ahead, color, but only inside the lines. So many rules, expectations, and underappreciation.

Those scripts, the ones that told us that being selfish for even a little while or taking care of ourselves was something that would need to wait until after everyone else is okay, they are ineffective and dangerous. As a clinician, I've seen women commit suicide because of overwhelming and healthy marriages murdered by the blade of expectation that one should come before the other. As a coach, I've seen both men and women become paralyzed with indecision when they needed to move forward by merely admitting what they truly wanted. As an advisor, I've seen them stuck, unfulfilled, and moving day to day on an auto-piloted survival mode rut that drains their life energy with every breath.

Enough is enough.

I hope that you read this book, take nuggets from every passage that applies to your life, and use it as confirmation of a time to do things differently. Break the scripts and binds of expectations, including your own outdated and weighted definitions. If you're living a story that helped you survive through some sort of mess in your life, but it's stunting your growth now, then use my words to help you break free. Old stories are good for lessons and growth, they are not to be repeated. It's time to be intentionally selfish and start putting yourself at the top of the list. The journey I share with you in this book is meant to help you embrace change and rewrite many folk-lores, including the notion that you must *seek to find* your peace and happiness. My life is a testament that you do not seek, and as my soul's half puts it, you **create to live and live to create** your own reality. So now, I implore you, in fact, I give you a little unsolicited permission to pause, live, laugh, and love your way to your joy.

# Section I:
# Permission to Pause

To those of us who insist on staying busy, note, there is a high toll to be paid when our energy fuse burns out. The price is non-negotiable, and its cost will be grave unless we accept an unsolicited but timely permission to pause.

# When Brilliance is Unbalanced

## 1

D epending on your circle of influence and your upbringing, my accomplishments over the past two decades may not necessarily win any awards in your book. If we would've set down over a cup of tea a few years ago, you would've had to pull the milestones out of me, and I would barely have admitted that they were feats worthy of being noted at all. Always moving, working, going, doing, I rarely slowed down to truly appreciate the very things I prayed for.

Over the years, some people have called me bright, while others went as far as telling me that I'm brilliant. I would always smile politely, feeling they had good intentions, so I'd nod, speak a soft acknowledging thank you while turning towards the back of my mind to check the Pandora's Box I buried long ago, just to make sure it was still under lock and key. "Brilliant!" I'd say to myself with a condescending chuckle. Thinking, "if only you knew…"

What most don't know is that the building blocks of my brilliance were infested with silent tears, trauma, and daily declarations spewed over me of how I was stupid and that I would "grow up to be 'nothing,' fast, and pregnant, just like my mother." The verbal blades cut deep. I understood very early in life that the people who hurt you the most would be those closest to you, often the ones charged to your care and guidance.

I remember when my grandmother gloatingly told me that my mother was tested when she was young, and she ranked off the charts as a genius, a mathematical genius to be exact. At times, I would hold onto that statement as an acknowledgment of my future potential, even though I sucked at math. I will admit that the statement would both plague my subconscious and comfort me when I was on a bit of an academically destructive path. You may ask why her being a genius would insight me to pull away from maximizing my potential. Well, the answer is simple, my mother, the genius, was a long *American Horror Story* episode of what life could or in the minds of some, should be. At the time of me writing/frantically editing this page, I'm a few weeks shy of 42 years old, and my mother has been heavily addicted to drugs and a life of manipulation, scheming, and full-on crime of one sort or another for over 33 years to date. Bound and buried gifts, that's what brilliance can look like when it's unbalanced.

I was raised in a house full of women who worked hard, multiple jobs, and never complained. They lived with their eyes wide shut to the unusual noises and open secrets that plagued our home. Everyone was always moving, going, doing, and being busy. I was what they would call the mouthy child. A scrawny toothpick little girl with the heart of a lion forced to quell my roar, so rebelliously, I yacked a lot. My ferocious side was smothered by daily threats of physical, sexual, and verbal abuse. Being bold was not applauded nor encouraged, it would most definitely get you beat down in my house. My natural propensity to speak what was on my mind was nearly extinguished after a few years of those open secrets. Then one day, divine intervention, wrapped in a rugged package of unexplainable disappointment, I felt pulled from the center of my core. The green hulk trigger was tripped, and it woke up my internal warrior.

There is something to be said about learned behavior, it's actually pretty difficult to unlearn when you have no context for where it originated from. It would take me years to understand that my tendency to despise dependency of any kind came from watching my mother break down because of it.

After three years of non-stop fighting with my father over infidelity and finances, followed by a few more years of trying unsuccessfully to sustain independence on her own, my mother moved us off Elaine Street. Having nowhere else to go, we went back into my grandmother's overcrowded Mt. Airy home, with one of her childhood abusers who would become yet another one of mine, her stepfather. I would later learn that he had abused my eldest uncle and my mother, both his non-biological children, in the basement until my Uncle ran away from home. Seeking a way to end her abuse, my mother intentionally conceived me knowing that it would cause shame on the family, and she'd be forced to get married and leave with some semblance of security via my emotionally broken father.

Although only 17 at the time, marriage would be her escape. Her stepfather wouldn't want anything to do with her now that she belonged to someone else, so her choice to carry a child would serve as the duality of carrying her to freedom. Or at least, so she thought. Just a few short years into living back in the red brick row home, my mother turned to crack cocaine before she was 24. In my grandmother's constant state of denial of all things outside of her control, she didn't notice or refused to acknowledge it, to this day, I'm still not sure which.

One day, in the early 80's, while playing in our joint closet, looking for 50cent pieces to snag, so I could get candy for the entire block (seriously, I've always been a giver)....- I found my mom's Louis Vuitton bucket bag pushed toward the back of the closet. Hair, nails, toes, and clothes, always polished. She was a very stylish, well put together woman, on the outside, all the time. My mother was extremely feminine, and she loved her pocketbooks. This bag, the one I decided to rummage through today, was one of her good ones. My interest peaked higher when I saw it stuffed behind the half empty tin cans of caramel popcorn. I quickly dug it out, curious to see how many 50 cent coins and perhaps even dollar bills, she might have stashed in there, unzipped it. As the golden zipper clasp broke apart to let me see what was inside, the first clue it gave me was when it unleashed a familiar nasty-sweet metallic smell. It's one I've smelled pretty regularly recently and had my suspicions of what it was. After all, this is the mid-80's and drugs were rampant. When I peeked inside, I found a brittle, whitish towel, stained with what looked like dirty fingerprints, as if someone had cigarette ash all over their hands before they touched it. A fairly curious cub, I unfolded the clunky, dirty towel, and found it filled with glass pipes, crack vials, and two neon colored lighters. We had the D.A.R.E bear (Drug Abuse Resistance Education) program in school, so I knew what I was looking at.

Just a few nights earlier, I remembered waking up to a flickering light going up the side of the wall and tasting something metallic in the back of my throat as I inhaled what was clearly toxic white crystals. This not being the first nor the 30th time it had happened, but in my sleepy bold haze, aggravated from being awakened by the chok-

ing smoke, I squealed, "ugh, mom, what is that smell?".
She must've been in her own haze because she didn't pop
me; instead, she pounded the wall with annoyance and
yelled for me to go back to sleep from her bottom bunk. I
remembered thinking, the next time, I'm climbing down
and catching her in the act! We'll see what she tries to deny then.

A few days past, but there was no nasty sweet smoke.
I thought I lost my chance to get proof. But here it was,
sitting in my mom's favorite brown and tan LV lettered
bag. So here it is, the divine intervention my spirit had
been signaling for. The trigger went off, my green hulk
warrior button was pushed, and I found instant strength
at that moment. I grabbed the undisputable bag of proof,
filled with glass vials and burnt towels. Marching down
the stairs, past the dark panel walls, I felt unconquerable.
At this very moment, I knew that no matter what other
secrets may exist in this house, this one would come to
light.

Understand, I loved my mother deeply, and I fully expected to get in trouble for snitching, smacked around,
cursed at a bit, put on punishment, and the like. I didn't
care. I wanted to help her, so I had to roar. Loud enough
so that the announcement couldn't be denied. All of the
eyes and ears in red brick houses would open to the reality that one of them was no longer able to cover her pain
behind her natural beauty. In my nine-year-old mind, I

had to save her. My mother was worth mustering the strength for. She would get the help she needed, and we would be able to leave this house of horrors immediately. She'd have to go to some sort of family rehab hospital, and perhaps, I'd get to go with her. Even if she couldn't take me immediately, as soon as she got out, she'd be well again, she'd get fixed, and we'd be able to live on our own, somewhere private and safe. In my nine-year-old mind, this moment, this risk I would take to help someone else, would be my personal remedy for the pain I'd been experiencing over my short life.

The plans of my heart, my good intentions, didn't quite work out the way I imagined that day. When I go to the bottom of the stairs, I took a deep breath, turned to the right to walk around our big slouchy couch, and in what would become my signature hype walk, I stomped my way towards the dining room where my grandmother was. I slammed the bag on the dining room table and stepped back a few paces. As expected, my grandmother, whose back was turned to me at the time, whipped her head around to ask me what on earth was I slamming things for. I said, "You should open it." As she glared in-to my eyes and saw my sharp stare returned to her, she got up and unzipped the bag. Immediately, she called for my step-grandfather. He came up from the basement in a huff. He was always looking for a good fight, regardless of who it was against. He ran up the stairs as if someone had broken into the house, he was ready to charge. I snickered a bit under my breath mostly because I looked forward to seeing him not be in control of something, anything.

My grandmother whispered something to him, I was standing right there but couldn't really hear, and maybe I didn't want to. He punched the table and started fussing at my grandmother. Shortly afterward, my mother came walking in the door from one of her jobs. I assume she was at the Wadsworth Checking Cashing job at the time because she got home rather quickly after my grandmother called. The adults made me go back upstairs for the first part of their discussion. I looked into my mother's eyes as I passed her to go up the stairs, and she looked disgusted.

I recognized that look, she had given it to me many times before. Usually, after I had made a mistake, spilled something on the floor, or asked a question about something I saw on television like the time I innocently asked, mom, "what are tampons?" She accused me of me fresh and said I already knew, she curled her lip up to the right, then glared at me as if I had just spit on her shoe. I honestly didn't know, but I would find out on my own a few days later when I snuck to the library. It was one of my latter scripts, if you want to know something, go research it.

In the seconds I had to look into my mother's eyes as I passed her, I was also receiving a highlighted message of disappointment. I didn't expect that, I thought she would be happy, at least relieved to know that help was on the way. Remember, my grandparents were a lot of things and did quite a few things wrong, but one thing they didn't do was deal with embarrassment. Presentation, expectation, and optics mattered to them. It had an unbalanced priority in their life, as long as no one was too intoxicated to recognize their humiliating behaviors. I knew they would not stand for my mother walking around our neighborhood copping drugs.

So, I went upstairs, feeling a bit heavy, unsure of what to do with those feelings that rushed over me when my mother glared deep into my eyes, so I paced in my room for about 5 minutes. Then I tried to listen through the floor ventilator. I couldn't hear, so I peep-toed out of my room towards the top of the steps. Crawled on all fours down the first few steps, being careful not to hit the creeks under the floorboard of the stairs, just far enough so I could hear. My mother denied everything at first, tried to say she was holding it for a friend. Of course, no one believed her. When she finally confessed, she did so a bit belligerently, arrogantly even. She told them to mind their business, it was her money, and her body and she could do what she wanted to do with it. My step-grandfather berated her, told her she had one choice. Either she stops today and goes into rehab, or she leaves.

Without hesitation, she stood up and said she's leaving. My grandmother pleaded with her to get help and take care of herself, telling her how important it was and how bad the drugs could get. My step-grandfather, whose face I couldn't see as I held on by my forearms from the stairs, said emphatically, "if you leave, you're not taking the girl with you." I jumped up, ran down the stairs, and into the dining room where they were all now standing. The large black, orange, and gold picture of the Philadelphia Bridge that hangs on the wall above the table seems to swallow the room. My mother looked at me, then back at her stepfather, and said, "fine, you keep her," as she turned and walked towards the stairs to go pack her things. I was numb. I couldn't move, I couldn't cry, my voice seemed stuck in my throat. Everything on my body was sore as if I had a simultaneous case of strep throat and the flu. Nothing felt real. With two exceptions.

Firstly, the intense feeling of failure was overwhelming all my senses, it was protruding through my gut, heart, and soul. I had one job, just one, to save my mother when she couldn't save herself. Secondly, I felt pulled by something bigger than myself, and I thought, very specifically, I would need to be at least seventy-five percent **different** than my mother and every other adult in my life at that time. I literally said out loud, "I WILL Be Differ-

But again, I was too young to understand the nuances of their adult relationship. Perhaps I was, in fact, being protected from something. I had my own memories of my father locking me in a small closet and leaving me there long enough to pee my pants more than once as I cried non-stop. Perhaps, there was more to his rage than I understood at the time. Losing his own mother to bacterial meningitis at 12 years old and dropping out of school in the 8<sup>th</sup> grade to help his family surely left a mark socially and developmentally. None of that was understood, nor did it matter at that moment. It had always been my mom, and I consistently to that point. Regardless of our mood swings, disappointing glares, and accusations about my innocence, it was always us. She broke her loyalty to me, and that pain was the most pronounced of the two.

The journey towards my purpose began here. I was jolted into a fixed space, a box of sorts, where my pattern of using my voice for others in need would be strengthened and ingrained over the next 30 years of my life. It would stir me towards my profession as a clinician and drive me deeper into the woods of understanding the cause, effect, and consequences of the decisions people make for themselves and in their relationships. It would be the driving force behind my incredible urge to provide a haven for my children, so much so that I would spend every waking moment building, working multiple jobs, going to school, earning degree after degree after certification after license and so on, so they would always have what they needed and could avoid the life I had been groomed in. If I couldn't fix my mother, I wanted to at least fix everyone and everything else around me, whether they were willing and ready, or not. I simply needed to help.

Those good intentions would take a ninety-degree pivot over twenty-two years later when my seven years and some month-old daughter looked at me one day across the dinner table and told me that she didn't like how I was treating her. She recounted how I didn't have patience with her during homework time and how forty-five-minute car rides to and from school, carpools to ballet class, soccer, and jazz weren't spending time with her. She told me I was awesome. She also told me I was awesome for everyone else but her. My daughter was calling me out and pointing out how the presentation and optics of our lives looked good to other people. We had a corner house in a suburb of Philadelphia, white picket fence, cute little puggle, 2.5 kids (yeah, I'll get to that later), and had been married at that point for nearly nine years. We "*looked*" great to someone peaking in through a peephole into our lives. But our reality, the widescreen view, was very different.

What I heard my daughter say at that moment was that I was brilliant and unbalanced. In my effort to build a life, relationships, and career, I got caught in running so far from my past that I ran straight into a twilight version of it. Although my children wouldn't experience a childhood laden with abuse or disturbing behaviors, in a misguided attempt to nurture them, I replaced it with overstuffed schedules and distractions to fill the void of my presence. I would love to say that I sprang into action immediately after the youngest of my children perfectly pointed out my glaring imperfection. But I didn't. The circle of colleagues and peers that I surrounded myself with at the time, held similar over-calendarized schedules for their children. It had become our normal way of doing what needed to be done in a day.

After nearly 2 years of mental restlessness, and being drained from my own internal battle, I took a look at how busy I was doing things and washed the *just learn how to be* pill that was lodged in my throat down with a bit of do it different liquid. Between the time I sat at the dinner table with my family and was punched in the inner child gut with the reality of my innocent but still hurtful wrong, my spirit and my ego were at war. Once I knew better, I began to do better, but I didn't want to move through life without sharing the simplest of discoveries, normal isn't necessary. It's why I'm committed to helping high-achieving, ambitious, brilliant women (and a few brave men) balance themselves, with their truth. You can't propel towards your destiny nor can you have healthy relationships if you're off balance. Countless documentaries have shown us that if you keep going at the speed of light, missing milestones, and not pausing to appreciate your achievements, you will absolutely run into the twilight version of everything you've said you'd never be. Those scripts of learned behavior will come back to bite you in the bottom, and if you're not vigilant, smother your dreams and ruin relationships with the people who matter most.

Ask me how I know.

# Loyal to a Fault

**2**

Throughout my early professional years, I created a pretty impressive list of saves both on and off the clock. In the beginning, I was hyper focused on children. Wanting to be a voice for the voiceless and protect them from situations like the one I grew up in. I developed great partnerships with other social workers, case managers, doctors, nurses, advocates, and tons of other helpers. All of us had our stories, our why's for what drove us into the field. Some were clearer on how they arrived in the underpaid lane of health and human services. Others were purposely avoiding trying to figure themselves out. I was a bit in between.

My resilience was often sparked by rebellion. I always felt strongest when I felt the pull to break out. Notice, I didn't say break free. That would indicate that I understood that I wasn't free, and to be honest, that would be something that would take me well into my late 30's to ascertain. But in my early years, I often would break out, mostly to help someone else. I was similar to a momma bear, even before I had kids. Pretty unassuming, quietly roaming, and minding my business, taking hits from nature and even other animals in the forest without too much more than a warning swipe. But, if you came near my proverbial cups, I'd break out of my normal calm and turn ferocious. This wasn't only reserved for family, but any friend that I considered close. I was and still, extremely loyal. Though, at those times, it was often to a fault.

## Trusting Gut Instincts

By the time I turned 11, my mother had been in at least three shelters, some stays shorter than others. I was still living in Mt. Airy with dark panels and looped wool carpet. My grandmother felt my behavior was becoming more pronounced, so she enrolled me in an all-girls Catholic Middle School, the one a couple of my younger aunts had also attended when the high school portion was still open. Although she was raising us as Jehovah's Witnesses, she felt the Catholic school nuns could do something with my attitude. She realized shortly after her first call to the school that they weren't ready for me either.

I wasn't a bad student, and I definitely wasn't a disobedient kid. I colored in the lines if you left me alone. It was only if you stepped too close to that edge we discussed before that I'd have a problem. The first time a nun hit me with a ruler because my skirt was an inch above my knee vs. at my knee, well that was an edge that I didn't know I had to warn her about. The second and final warning my grandmother received from the school was the day another young lady stole something from one of the teachers and put it in my bookbag when the nuns did an open bag check. I was the only public-school transplant in our all-girls' catholic school. All of the other girls had been together since Kindergarten and knew each other fairly well.

The immediate consensus when the teacher, Mrs. Wright's wallet went missing, was that the public school girl had stolen it. I absorbed their projection, processed it, and then spit it out. I wasn't worried when they announced the book bag checks. I had stolen plenty of times before but always from someone who pissed me off. Mostly, $20 bills from my step-grandfathers pants pocket and tons of quarters and 50 cent pieces from my mother's popcorn tin when she lived with us. But I hadn't taken anything from Mrs. Wright. She was the only non-nun instructor we had, an African American woman with style and grace, and I liked her. I knew in my gut they thought it was me, but it didn't matter, because I was innocent. Part of my rebellious nature was to be fine with being caught at any wrong I'd done, and often, I'd own up to it. With a defiantly nonchalant stance, but I'd own up to it. I refused to be blamed for anything that I didn't do, though. That was off the table.

The nuns told us to unzip our bags and place every-thing on the table, leaving the bag on the floor near our feet. We all complied. A few minutes before the inspectors were due to come to our table, the girl across from me, bent down and I felt a slight rustle from my bag near, which was leaning at the tip of my black and white ox-ford shoes. I looked down but didn't see anything odd, so I went back to chatting with the girls to the left of me. We were all anxious to get over this so we could go to recess.

As the inspections progressed around the room, I would occasionally glance over at the young lady across from me, she was sweating across her brow. Her curly dark brown hair had started to frizz a bit near the edges of her scalp where the beads of sweat were gathering. Her twin sister was in the room at another table. I looked over at her, but she was engaged in conversation, clearly obliv-ious to any happenings at our table. When the nuns came to our table, they looked through the piles of books and pencil cases on top of the table, then began to search our bags, which were instructed to be empty. They looked at hers, a sigh of relief went across her face, then a smirk. I jumped up and stared deeply into the soul of the girl across from me, flaming with thoughts of punching her smirk through the back of her head. In that instant, I felt a powerful confirmation in my spirit that she set me up. The nun, Sister Catherine, who I had already had ruler-run-in with, sternly told me to take my seat before reaching for my bag. My heart pounding out of my chest, I tried to wait for what I knew was coming. She dug her hand into the large open space, pulled out Mrs. Wright's wallet, and shook her head. As she reached down to grip my arm and tell me to go to the office, I leaped across the table and grabbed the girls' throat. I refused to let go as she struggled to breathe, and the teachers, nuns, and students tried to break my hands-free. I remember yelling, cursing, and saying every explicative I could think of at that moment. I went from a smiling 70 lb. eleven-year-old and turned into an uncontrollable animal.

I don't remember how, but at some point, I let go. I stared deeper into that girl's soul and told her to tell the truth as they pulled me back and pushed me through the doors to go to the headmaster's office. She confessed. But I was still in trouble. I've now been classified as a danger to others, defiant, disobedient, and relentless in my pursuit of truth. All traits I'd learn to love about myself later. But today, I was 11, and I was simply a misfit.

My grandmother was called and told that they would refund her my tuition and strip the balance of my scholarship if I had any other outburst. They said that I was a safety threat for the other girls, and it wouldn't be tolerated. My grandmother didn't care that I was accused of stealing, she cared that I embarrassed her. So, she made me a deal, one I'd be happy to take. She said I could stay at the school, she'd continue to pay my tuition, but I needed to go live with my mother in South Philly. I was simply too much for her to handle.

I trusted my gut instinct about the other girl, and I was right, but my strong intuition and lack of capacity to manage my emotions hadn't saved me, it instead turned me into a combustion agent. As an adult, I'd learn just how powerful my gifts would become once I'd gain control of my emotions. But at 11 years old, I could only make myself a promise, one that I've held on until this day and apply to my adult environments as applicable. "Kia, always trust your gut, but when it can be avoided, kick-ass after school and not in it so the innocent will be safe from your wrath..."

## Seeking to Seal Broken Bonds

I'm sure you can imagine, I had mixed feelings and reservations about moving in with my mother. First off, she was still in a shelter at the time my grandmother told me it was time to go. She was staying at the Salvation Army Shelter in their family division, awaiting her section 8 housing approval. She was pregnant with my baby brother and shared a dorm size room with another family. Prior to her pregnancy, I'd visited my mother in other shelters, dank, dark, grey jail cell walls, with the feeling of just as much safety as you could expect in a general population prison. Hardly any. I'd also slept in alley ways and crack houses with her before she got desperate enough to deal with a shelter and all its rules in the first place. A major plus of me moving in was that now she qualified as a family and would be moved up the list to get her housing voucher earlier. I knew in my gut that it was one of the primary reasons she was so willing to take me in. Over the years, I've come to learn quite a lot about my mother's manipulation and cutthroat survival mode tactics. At the time, I didn't care much. I was seeking a relationship, I wanted her to want me and not to be disappointed. I wanted her loyalty, and I was adamant about showing her mine.

Shortly after I was added to her voucher as an additional dependent, we moved to South Philly. A rather large brownstone off 15th and Wharton Street, with whitewashed marble stone steps and a thin metal railing that divided our home from the house on the left. This block was long and much wider than any of the blocks I was familiar with in Mt. Airy. Across the street from our home sat an all-white house with huge red felt bows at the base of every window. I would later come to know the owner of that house, not personally, but as part of my intimate window watching. There was always a fancy black car pulled up to the house, and the brown skinned woman who would get in would typically greet a different man each time. I'm not positive about her real name, but as a kid, we called her Star. The name stuck for me because she seems to dress and live like we would assume a movie star would. Always appearing hood photoshoot ready, often laced with eccentric outfits and big wigs. When I think back to all of the drama that happened in front of, and sometimes through the windows of her home, Star's life was my first reality television series. Not that I needed anyone else's drama on-screen nor in real life, but hey, it served as a distraction.

I digress. When we moved into the brownstone, we rented the top two floors of the three-story building. It was like living in a house that set above a large apartment. I had the entire third floor to myself. A nice size bedroom with high ceilings and windows that sat only a foot above the floor. They were both a bit scary and beautiful to look at. I'd never seen windows so tall before. Once I had my bed, I'd have a large window on either side of the bedpost. There was also a smaller room adjacent to mine. We didn't actually need that room per se' as we didn't really have any furniture. It was sort of cool to have one right next to mine, especially since it had a working sink. Yeah, there was a small sink, similar to one that would sit on the wall in a small powder room, except this one just protruded from the wall. No mirror or cabinets around it, just the sink and the pipe that looped from the base back and up into the wall. A bit odd, but hey, it was ours. My mother and now new baby brother's room set on the 2nd floor, just below the third-floor stairs. There was one small bathroom, and the kitchen and living room were designed as an open floor plan, so it served as the anything space.

South Philly was a new world for me. I met some amazingly spirited kids and was once again the outsider. At the time, I was fresh blood. The young, light skin, thin frame, sandy brown hair girl with the big forehead and large nose. You couldn't tell me I wasn't the toughest thing walking. Until the first time I got jumped, because I was so bull headstrong, I interpreted that moment, especially since I didn't take the beating lying down, as a declaration that I could handle anything, being jumped and coming out with no broken bones included. Most tweens would've bowed down and bowed out. Nope, my scripts were set. It was merely another aspect of my life that I'd either get used to or get over it. Fortunately for me, although there were quite a few single fights here and there, I was never jumped again. It may not have mattered much to my younger, bull headed self, though as an adult, I am thankful that I didn't have to keep proving to myself that I could handle being jumped by six-plus people simply for walking on the wrong street and not being from that block. Some lessons don't need to be repeated.

A few weeks after, I moved to South Philly, I met a few kids from the DeVose Family. I learned quickly that they were incredible people, tight knit, caring, protective, humble, smart, and cautious. Their family was huge, to say the least. If memory serves me correctly, their grand-mother had 17 children, and all of those children had nice size families as well. Many of them lived within blocks, sometimes doors of each other. I was in love with how much love they seem to share. It was then that I'd be in-troduced to how unusual my family was. Not the fact that my grandmother had raised me or that my mother had a drug addiction. This was the 80's, so that wasn't an ex-treme revelation.

The fact that I had to cart my six-month-old baby brother around with me everywhere, nearly all the time, and that I could stay out until 4 am raised a few eye-brows. To be honest, none of those things was my normal coming from my grandmother's house either. It was as if the pendulum swung from hard left to the far right over-night. My grandmother didn't allow me to do anything! No company in the house, not even my younger three sib-lings, which made bonding with them the way I'd connect with my youngest brother so much more difficult. If I could sit on the step and laugh with a few friends without her telling me to quiet down outside, that was a good day. Whereas my mother just wanted me to handle her kid and stay out of her way. Many of those nights I was "al-lowed" to stay out was because we were locked out of the apartment. My mother was inside having one of her par-ties, so I needed to ship the crying six-month-old with me on my hip or in his stroller elsewhere until people started leaving, which was normally around four in the morning. These could be weekdays or weekends. It just depended on what day the 1st of the month fell on. That's when the food stamps and cash got picked up from the county assistance office.

I made the best of it. Sometimes I'd walk with my brother back to the places I'd been to earlier with friends, down to Passyunk Avenue, passed all the closed shops and stores. Other times we'd walk towards the supermarket where the sign was still lit to avoid all the dark of night. Occasionally, of the kids from the side of the DeVose family that lived across the street from our brownstone would be up, and she'd sneak outside to sit on her stoop with me. She was the youngest of eight in that house, a bit of risk-taker, and simultaneously a calm spirit. We'd talk about how odd it was that I had to sit outside so late. If the conversation got too heavy, we'd just started talking about all the other fools on the block. Many of them were my mother's new best friends, especially around the first of the month.

This might all sound bad, but those were regular days for me. They weren't anything close to the bad days I was used to either. I made the most of what I had and tried to enjoy a little innocent wild fun in during those years as well. Occasionally, I'd get a chance to sit on marble stone stoop with a boy I liked. I had my first real kiss that first summer. It was a big difference from being in mount airy.

I didn't have to worry about my grandmother coming outside and embarrassing me, calling me through the window for me to get across the street like I just blew a hole in something. I went from extremely sheltered, in terms of what I could do, and where I could go. To have more freedom than even I could or should've needed to handle. Fortunately, I was a good girl at heart. I intentionally stayed away from drugs, drinking, and smoking. My #1 vice back then was the same one I would eventually struggle with throughout my adult years, being so focused on wanting people to live to the potential I could see in them, instead of meeting them where they were and letting them be who they kept showing me they had always been...

I had thoughts of how easy it would be if I just let go, put my inhibitions aside, and just picked up one of the various things I would often see on my mother's dresser. But I was afraid. Literally of myself. I didn't want to lose control and not be able to get back to me. A script that stayed with me for decades to come. Besides, my mother was careless enough for the both of us. One time she caught me looking at a beer can; it was an Independence Day block party. Perhaps I was contemplating that day, or maybe she thought I was- I don't really remember, but I do know she called for me from outside where I stood with my girlfriends. She told me to come into the apartment. We went to the second floor, Ms. Niecey, our neighbor downstairs was there. My mother stood in the kitchen in from of our neighbor and poured a whole BIG 20oz. cup of St. Ides Malt Liquor. Now, mind you, I'm all of, at this point, I'm just 24 days shy of my 13th birthday. She pours this drink and makes me drink it. I said no several times, and she kept insisting, saying "no, I'd rather you have your first glass of beer with me than out there in the street getting into some kind of trouble."

Of course, I'd never tasted beer before. It smelled horrible, it looked disgusting, and I hated it. It tasted like what I would imagine urine to taste like it was carbonated. Note, I don't drink beer, or anything carbonated today.... Now I don't say this to point out my mother's horrible judgment as a parent. In her own way, she was trying to teach me a lesson that she hoped I'd learn from. I will admit, it did the trick for the most part. It made me never to want beer again. Can't say it didn't make me want anything else, but it definitely made me never want beer again.

Except for one moment in my early teens when a friend convinced me that I was missing out on trying other types of alcohol, the kind with no carbonation, the syrupy sweet one called sex on the beach. Well, that had me vomiting for two hours, so that was it for me. I honestly never drank alcohol again until I was 30 years old. The power of scripts. They can work for you or against you. In this case, the script to not lose control had me so close to the edge of temptation just a few years after my mother's test, that I convinced myself to try it again, just "more like juice," from what they told me. It took one bad taste at nearly 13 and one bad experience at nearly 16 for me to ban it from my life for 15 years. I had a rule, I'd wear eye makeup and have my first glass of wine after I was 30. Except for forced make up for proms or hair photoshoots, that's exactly what I did. When I'm loyal to a person, place, or thing, I'm locked in until damn near death. Literally, loyal to a fault.

My friends thought my mother was bizarre because they had parents who *wouldn't* give them beer, and mine just made me, forcefully, drink it. I came outside, I couldn't stop peeing. I had to keep running back and forth in the house to use the restroom. I was fatigued, delirious, silly, nauseous, and completely out of control. I determined that beyond the strangeness of the introduction to alcohol, I was clearly a human that couldn't hold liquor and self-determined that I was a true lightweight. I was around enough drinkers to know that little 12oz can shouldn't have made me loopy.

I could've resisted my mom. Truly, but I was seeking a moment to seal our bond. It had been broken for so long, and I had been waiting for a way back in. She was pretty jovial that night. Partially because she was riding her high at that point in the evening. Most of the neighbors were out partying, the crabs were seasoned, people were sitting on the stoop, with newspaper on their laps and trying not to trip over the water bowl separated for the sole use of dipping the "mustard" off the crabs before dousing them in hot sauce. The adults had plenty of 40oz bottles and six-packs of beer, lots of marijuana, cigarettes, and music that summer.

Needless to say, my mother and I did not bond that summer. In fact, our relationship became more strained. As much as I'd tried to jump in and help, even without being asked, she'd still look at me with disgust in her eyes. I was cursed at and cursed out daily. I started to look forward to coming home and finding her passed out. Those were days there was a bit of peace in the house. The challenge of course, was knowing my brother was never safe at home with her. There were days I'd come home and find him alone, crawling around in his room in a filthy diaper and milk all over the place. She wasn't there, but at least she put the baby gate up I'd mumble. The worse days were when there'd be a random guy in the apartment. Smug and arrogant, young, not too much older than me. I knew what they were and why they were there. I just got to the point that I'd block out her ridiculousness and momma bear over my brother. I started taking him everywhere I went. People would look at me and assume he was my spawn. I was used to the glares of disgust at home, so I really wasn't fazed by their ignorant assumptions. My pain was something they couldn't touch, and it ran deep.

The scripts of abandonment, lack of attachment, not enough, unworthiness, failure, people pleasing, and the fear of my personal power were not created that first summer in South Philly. They were merely deepened, anchored to my subconscious with a sophisticated heaviness that would take me more than three years of therapy, development of an intimate relationship with God, and a divorce to repair.

For years to come, I'd enter relationships that were meant to be a blip on the screen, short-lived lessons that would overrun their stay and become nightmares. All because I wanted to save the other person or at least stay long enough to fix something so they could finally see how great I saw them. Showing up in each relationship with full trust given though not yet earned was a signature staple. I left no room for myself to get to know someone outside of what my heart whispered, often ignoring my gut unless there was an immediate perceived threat.

I was right back to that seventh-grade classroom at the beginning of every relationship. All smiles and laughs, regardless of projected assumptions. As long as I knew I wasn't doing anything wrong and they didn't show any visible signs of mistrust, no hypothetical beads of sweat across their brow, there was no reason to lean into what I would later understand as my spirits warning. The reason? Because I wanted to jump in as fast as possible, to begin the relationship, and have another opportunity to correct previous failures via this new person problem.

My strong intuition and positive energy would pull people towards me, they'd feel connected to me nearly instantly, allowing for us to bond quickly and bypass some of the normal trust-building filters that most people get stuck behind. I couldn't always explain it, but it was an influential wave of energy that I'd learn to use for the good of others. The challenge of my youth was seeing this intuitive tool as a way to prove my worth, to show that I was enough. So instead of learning to understand my gift, to listen to my intuition when it would warn me that these relationships would become toxic if I continued in them, to let go and move on, I'd simply become loyal to a fault.

# Rewarded Regrets

## 3

Over the next few years, I'd live through a series of unfortunate events in and around that South Philly brownstone. It was in this house that I learned how far I was willing to go to protect the ones I loved, eventually, including myself. The layers of trauma that would be stacked like dominos would lead me to pause and make a decision that would change the course of my life forever. After a few years of parenting my mother, it would be within these open brick walls and narrow hallways that I would choose to be selfish and take care of myself, going against the nerve in my body that told me not too. One of the hardest decisions I'd make in my life, I made the week of my 15th birthday, and it saved my life. But of course, it would take me a few years of limited thinking, doubting my potential and moving through my torture with blinders of naivety before I'd get to that point....

Mr. Eddie, who was my mother's boyfriend at the time, was at least 25 years her senior, brought the winter with him. I remember the first time he walked his 350 plus pounds, dirty car oil smell up my third floor stairs. I had just finally gotten Robby to sleep after a tough teething spell. There was absolutely nothing on that floor that belonged to anyone but me and no reason for any adult outside of my mother to march up those steps. But here he was, sitting next to me on my bed as I'm laying down on my belly watching my little 13in TV with the antenna sticking up. I got up to maneuver the antenna to get a better signal, calculating which I could get to fastest, the knife I kept on the other side of my bed, or my backpack where I kept my large metal scissors. In the event that I needed to slice something, I wanted to be prepared to cut deep and cut quickly.

He started talking about how he understood that I needed money sometimes, and how my mom doesn't always have it because she's not working consistently. Then he flipped his tone a bit more aggressively and started to iterate that my mom told him that I had jobs when I lived with my grandmother, so I was old enough now to understand how I can't keep expecting things for free while I'm living here with "them." He pressed that I would need to do my part and work to help pay bills. As I sat there half listening (more so, watching his every physical movement), I thought to myself, "what is this man talking about, nobody in this house gives me anything. Most of my clothes were given to me by my aunts that are 8-12 years older than I am, or I buy what I can from babysitting the downstairs neighbor's kids..." I've always had some kind of under the table job since I was 12. From shampoo girl at a local hair salon, running errands for neighbors, to whatever else was on the up and up that I could get paid cash for where I could take my baby brother with me. There weren't too many options with for a 12-year-old with a six-month old being totted around in a faded blue, banged up umbrella stroller. But I made it work for my school tokens, some snacks for me and my brother, and to give my mother towards bills as a deterrent for her selling her body.

At least a half dozen times, prior to this moment, Mr. Eddie would occasionally take my brother and me with him on various appointments around town where he had to help someone repair a car. He was known around the area as a neighborhood mechanic. His energy always made me a little skeevy, but outside of lying and telling people we were his kids, he had never made me feel in danger before his night. On those trips, he'd often ask me to hold his toolbox, hand him a rag or screwdriver, something or other, and he'd give me $2-5 for being his "little assistant." Yet, another reason I didn't understand what he meant by those statements about pulling my weight. Until he got close to me... he moved over on the bed and said his back hurt; he told me to massage his neck. I jumped up and said, "ewwww, no." Beyond the obvious inappropriateness of it all, he smelled like mechanic oil, grease, and dirt. His fingernails were marred with dark black streaks of car residue and disgusting. He was fat, old, and smelled like he ran a marathon after he rolled around in dog sweat. There was no way I was touching him!

I remembered standing there, only a few feet away from where I kept my knife under the right side of the mattress, thinking to myself, "Why would you want me to touch you? I'm a freaking kid! What are you talking about?! Go downstairs to my mother for that. You're being a PIG!" Unfortunately for him, those were things that I actually said outside of my head. I didn't realize how loud I was until I heard my brother crying downstairs. Back then, I definitely had a mouth on me. Anyone who knew me knew that much. He clearly didn't know me at all. Mr. Eddie looked at me, chuckled it off in a way that felt a bit like a warning, he got up off the bed and closed the door.

Now, I'm no stranger to this, unbeknownst to him. I'm no stranger to feeling locked in, boxed in, or feeling like I had no escape. I'm also no stranger to fighting, so I was prepared. One of us was going to go out that third-floor window, I knew that much. And I was hoping that I could push his big, fat, smelly, nasty behind so hard he'd fly through Star's window across the street. Fortunately, for both of us, that night didn't go as far as I thought he was trying to get it to go. When he closed the door, I immediately told him that he needed to open it and that he needed to get out of my room. Mr. Eddie, this clearly over 55-year-old man, took a breath, then in the calmest, deepest, the eeriest voice I've ever heard said, "yeah, but not before you give me a backrub." I argued with him a bit, tried to get loud, and even kicked the metal frame of the bed, trying to make some noise, hoping to get my mother's attention from right below us. She never came upstairs. Ok, she's high out of her mind, which is exactly why he came upstairs to talk to me in the first place. I realized the confirmation I had hope wasn't true. Those skeevy feelings that I used to have when I was around him on his mechanic trips with my brother, they were in fact my gut feeling that this dude was a full-on creep.

He comes in closer, and he said, "I'm not leaving until you rub my back." I keep saying, "are you serious, no," and he keeps haggling me like we're on 52nd street at one of the hat guy stands. "Oh, I'll give you $5.00, ok, I'll give you $10.00..." As the moments continue, I'm getting angrier by the second. In my heart, I think I can take him like physically dominate this huge grown man and win... I yell for the final time, "I don't want your money, and I want you to get out of my room." He stepped back just slightly, stares into my eyes, and said, "You know if you don't rub my back then I'm going down to your brother's room."

I immediately felt helpless. It didn't matter that only a few seconds ago, I was so mentally positive that my little 75lb self could slice his 350 plus pounds to shreds by pure will. I knew my brother, who I knew my mother would leave in the care of this dude when I was in school or the few minor occasions, I was with friends without him, couldn't protect himself. I'd die for my brother, I'd kill for my brother, I'd also sacrifice myself and the little innocence I had left to save his. I told my mother's boyfriend to sit down. He had me by the heart, knowing I would never risk my brother being hurt.

Mr. Eddie laid down on my small twin bed, took off his shirt, and exhaled. I climbed on the back of him, trying my best to straddle in a way that I could jump up and run if needed. This was the first time I envisioned myself killing someone. I kept thinking, "I have scissors in my bookbag lying against the wall. If I could get to them, I could stab him in his neck..." Then he grunted, "come on, get to work." I stretched my left hand out in front of me, shaking, but only slightly. As I reached to touch his neck, I felt acid in my throat, I was literally about to throw up. I kept trying to hold myself together. I can't throw up and get to the scissors in my bookbag... There's no way I can do both. For me, vomiting was always a violent scene. I hated it whenever I had the flu and had to vomit, it was worse than all the other stuff that came with it. There's no way I could let myself throw up. Not now.

For about three to four minutes, I went through a whole plot on how to get to my scissors, stab him in his neck, run to grab my brother, his diaper bag, milk, our coats, and run away to my aunt and uncle's house that lived a few blocks away off 17th and Annin Street. They had no idea what I was dealing with over in the brownstone, and to be honest, I knew that if I told them, my mother might not ever be seen again. They were good people, they loved me, and I knew they wouldn't stand for the nonsense. I also knew that I would regret not seeing my mother again, at least that year.

So here I was, massaging him for those 3-4 minutes while I disappeared into my mental movie of how to get away with murder, and save my baby brother. He made a noise that reminded me of one my step-grandfather used to make on those nights he'd make me sleep in his bed. I damn near had a heart attack, jumped in the air, falling off the bed, I yelled, "Alright, I'm done." He was like "that's it?" He tried to convince me to go lower, he needed more. I screamed at him as thunderous as I could to just get out of my room. Mr. Eddie, who then became Eddie the Creep, smirked. I knew right then and there what this process was, because again unbeknownst to him, I'm no stranger to what I would later learn to know and call a grooming process.

Regrettably for him, I was a little bit savvier, wiser and a little bit angrier from my past trauma. At this stage, it wasn't about screaming and fighting for some attention to get someone to recognize what was going on and hoping that they would come help or rescue me. This was about survival, and if only one of us was going to leave that room whole, it was going to be me. I refused to be a prisoner to fear so I told myself I would have to be the aggressor, I was going to kill him, and I was prepared to do so. If for nothing else, to save my brother from going through the same torment that I went through.

One thing was made very clear to me on this unlucky night. I was a target. Like a bunny whose flesh had been ripped from a previous attack during a fight with one animal and now every animal in the vicinity could smell fresh blood and dart towards it. I thought, there was no way in the world other kids my age were going through this, over and over again. Or so I thought.

Eddie, the Creep got up, put his shirt on, and told me "you can tell your mom if you want to, she's not going to believe you." I said "it's alright. I don't have to worry about telling my mom anything, I can handle myself, you just better not EVER touch my brother, or I will kill you." In my mind I was convinced that I had been through the worst, and it was nothing else that anybody could do, and if that little 3 or 4 minutes could get him out of my room, then so be it. Of course, after he left, I had somewhat of a cry-down, I won't say breakdown, but a cry-down. I called my girlfriend from around the corner, and she confirmed that it's not normal, he was in fact creepy and kept telling me that I needed to tell an adult and that this shouldn't be happening. I said "yeah, I know, but what am I going to do? My mom isn't going to leave him, and if she does, she's just going to replace him with the next jerk, who's also going to be a freak". I didn't tell her about my airy mount past, but I definitely felt like I needed to vent just a little bit about that episode, and I felt from her response that she was probably going to tell someone, which was going to cause more drama. So, I decided right then and there that I wasn't going to tell her anything else when it came to that. So even in the future, when she asked, I just kind of kept it to myself and wouldn't share and say, "everything's fine, everything's fine."

As I expected the next night when my mom got high, he tried to come up stairs. I heard him coming. I had Robby up there with me, so I decided that we were going to climb out on the roof where his old, fat, nasty self would never venture. So that's exactly what we did. Out the third-floor window in the back room with that stupid sink, and straight to the roof. We sat on the roof for a couple of hours until I saw his car pull off. I didn't know at the time, but the roof would become my haven for the next two years.

## Creepy Turns Crazy Red

Just as I had predicted in my little pre-teen mind, Eddie the Creep grew tired of my mother's drug addict behavior. Her constant stealing from him on top of lying when she had other men in the house to sell her drugs, trade her body, or sell them the furniture Eddie the Creep bought when he called himself moving in, he was fed up, so he finally left. He moved around the corner to his mother's house. Clearly, the distance was enough to make my mother feel comfortable moving her next Creep in. Now in comes Mr. Red. Red was the woman down the street, Ms. Carol's brother. The mom of those two little kids, Muda and Raymond, little chubby over-weight, emotionally abused, physically aggressive children. Red was a whole new level of creep. He had been to jail a few times and had just the right amount of wrong flavoring him crazy, so that's what I dubbed him, Crazy Red.

One would think by this point, that I'd just run away, report my mother to Children & Youth, or at least tell one of my aunts. Well remember, although the glimmer of hope is fading, I am still hopeful that my mother's spell will be broken. That she'll snap out of her drug medicated haze and choose to live right for both of her children. The thought came up often, did we matter, were we enough for her to do better? Of course, I couldn't' answer this question, or perhaps I didn't want to. Instead, I anchored onto hope that when she finally gets it together, she'll look at me with pride in her eyes, instead of disgust. When she awakes from this living nightmare, she'll thank me for holding things down, taking such good care of my brother, for fixing so many things along the way, and not failing. She'll be thrilled that I survived, not just for myself, but for all of us. She knows I'll forgive her for all the days I had to walk from South Philly to Chestnut Hill to school because she stole my tokens and found all the various hiding spots for my money. She loves me deeper because I haven't abandoned her and shared all her shameful secrets with our judgmental family members. She'll be proud that I was such a good secret keeper, and my reward will be her loyalty from that moment until forever...

On Tuesday morning, as I rushed down the third-floor stairs to get my cheap dollar store body spray so I could head to school, I was met by Red and his Creepy Crazy at the foot of the stairs. The entrance to my mother's bedroom is right there, so he just stood in the doorway, staring at me. As I bounced down the steps in my gray skirt, knee-high burgundy wool socks, and black and white oxford laced shoes, I could see my mother's feet hanging over her bed. I knew what they had been doing, as always. Her body looked as limp as a noodle. My stomach clenched, I paused on the stairs, for a quick second I wondered, "Is she dead?" But the eeriness I felt wasn't death, it was a familiar danger.

Crazy Red looked at me and said, "You know, I'm a little tired today, but I'm also getting tired of her. She's starting to not be too good for me anymore. Next trip is upstairs". Those words BURNED through my heart because the look in his eyes was a look of prophecy. It was like nothing I had ever seen before. I almost felt like his eyes had turned red, and I could see right through to this evil thing that was living within him. That moment made me feel like I would never be safe again in my life... He didn't touch me, he didn't yell, he didn't curse, he didn't smirk either, but at that moment, it was so clear and so evident, he already saw exactly what he planned to do to me. I heard my friends' voice in my head, telling me to just tell someone. I convinced myself to tell my mom about it, thinking, "You know what? She hasn't known this man long, it's got to be some piece of protection in her that wants her to intervene, something-somewhere-somehow."

The next lucid moment she had was when I got home from school that afternoon. I told her how I really didn't feel comfortable around him. I told her how he looks at me and what he said to me that morning. She looked at me and said, "it's not like you're a virgin anyway."

Any bit of respect that I had for my mother, anything residual craving for a bond that I had left inside of me literally spilled out of my soul instantly. At that very moment, on the foot of her bed, on the 2nd floor of our south

Philly brownstone was when I began to despise my mother. I loved her every flaw prior to that moment. I could justify, reason, explain a way, and cover up anything she'd ever done to me or around me before that day. Before that very instant, I had always held on to the possibility that she didn't know what was happening to me in Mt. Airy. That somehow, she was duped or drugged, or even just slept that hard and never knew. I would lean into the short sporadic memories I had from when I was around 4 or 5 years old, and she'd play Luther Vandross on the record player, make me fresh salads and treat me to my favorite ice cream, strawberry cream, after I'd eaten all my vegetables when we lived in our apartment on Elaine street. I didn't have many good wholesome memories, but that was one I held on to. But ice cream, veggies, music, and a few laughs weren't going to fix this. That day, everything changed. It was the day she lost her daughter, and I never trusted her to be anything more than what she was at that moment again.

After that, I became increasingly aggressive with my mother. Disrespectful doesn't describe what I evolved. If she looked at me, I jumped in her face. If she got in my face, I'd push her back. We even got to the point that we began to tussle with each other. Never a closed fist or open hand, but I had no respect for her after that moment. I became extra aggressive with her in the most insolent way that any child can become outside of putting my hands on her. I no longer looked at her as my mother, or even as an adult that deserved an ounce of respect. She was now, just another threat, someone else who was out to destroy my flesh and treat like wounded prey. I was now the one who was disgusted.

I had befriended a few of the neighborhood dealers who liked the fact that I could make the laugh, was tiny, and they thought it was dope how I always cared for my brother, even though they sold smack to my mom. I was tiny, hadn't come into any shape yet, so there was no physical attraction for most of them, so they called me their "little sister." I leveraged that one day and told them about the creeps and crazies like Red, who were trying to get at me through my mom. A couple of them gave me their pager number and said, just put in 911 and your address, and we'll handle it if it ever happens again. I paged them on Red the Creepy Crazy the next time I saw him glance my way. I didn't see him again for three weeks. When I did, his face was all lumped up, and he wouldn't look at me. I felt good about that for a few days, but my mother was getting ridiculous with these random dudes. I didn't want to extend my thug resource over too much, so I was careful not to call unless I really couldn't handle things.

Over the coming months, my mother's drug habit got worse. She progressed to heroin and added drunken recklessness to her behavioral resume. She became desperate to feed her increasingly incessant habit. She actually started sending people to the house while I was there alone with my brother. She would leave, and 5-15 minutes later, the doorbell would ring.

I'd go to my 3$^{rd}$ floor window to look out, there would be a strange man outside who would say, "your mom said I could come in." I was like, I'll be damned...and of course, I wouldn't let them in, and I would go up on the roof with my brother just in case they tried to break in. That routine got old and dangerous rather quickly. It was wearing on me emotionally, physically, and spiritually. But more importantly, my baby brother was walking and running now. I couldn't risk him pulling away from me while we were on the roof.

I was frustrated and starting to become a little scared because I knew that as fast as I was when I ran on my own, I could only go so fast with a toddler in my arms. Someone would catch me. Hell, my mother might even purposely open the door for someone and let them in my room while I was sleeping. I was a late bloomer, but I knew I'd be growing into my body sooner or later, and the dope boys weren't always going to look at me as a little sister... I had to be really mindful of how often I was willing to page one of them before they started asking for some sort of favors in return. I couldn't afford to risk it. I was tired of hiding tokens and money on the wall. I was tired of her selling my sneakers and clothes. I was tired of not knowing what or who I was going to come home to. Whether it be 3:00 pm or 4:00 am in the morning. I was tired of sitting outside all night. The winters were cold, and the summers were hot. Heck, even the bugs were creeping me out. South Philly had flying cockroaches that would come out at night, and that alone was making me insane. To this day, I can barely deal with anything larger than a fly zipping past my head.

## The 1st Selfish Save

I had to make a decision, the biggest one I'd had to make so far, and it was between two horrible options. My step-grandfather had died the summer before, so I had known for a while that my grandmother would welcome me back in. But there were two key issues that needed to be addressed. First, my grandmother's unspoken mental health problems had gotten progressively worse since her husband died. Second, she had already told my mother that she could not and would not raise another grandchild. With my step-grandfather gone, I knew I would be physically safe. I knew I would eat every day because there would be no one stealing my money, nor burrow holes I'd need to create to hide it in. I also knew I would have heat in the house every day because if there was anything I knew for certain; it was my grandmother never liked being cold.

So, one afternoon, I called my grandma, and I asked her if I could come home. Mind you, I left as a pretty belligerent and prideful teenager. She asked me what was going on. I didn't get into the nitty-gritty details; instead, I summed it up by telling her my mom was doing "that stuff" again, and things were so hard that I needed to leave and really wanted to bring my brother. In fact, I'm sure I told her that I needed to bring him desperately. For reasons that I would understand later, but not at the time, my grandmother iterated that I could come, but he couldn't. She didn't have the same bond with my brother that she obviously had with me, because she pretty much raised me, but she also felt and said if I take my brother from my mom than she has absolutely no reason to get her life together.

At 15, I thought that was disturbing. Like, why would you want your grandson to go through anything just for the sake of your daughter possibly one day, someday getting her life together? Why would you not help him too? It took me a few days before I could convince myself to leave him because I knew that I would be leaving him in the hands of someone who wasn't capable. But I also knew I was on the road to jail, or being put under one, because I had visions of my future that were linked to living with my mother if I did, I was going to kill someone. If it wasn't my mother, it was going to be one of those men she was letting in the house. So reluctantly, tearfully, horrified, at leaving my brother, not wanting to let him go. I took a deep breath, packed my bags, kissed my baby brother goodbye, intentionally and selfishly saved myself.

I moved back in with my grandmother in the redbrick mount airy home — a mature yet extremely torturous decision, crucial for both of us. I would find out later that my grandmother was suffering with mental illness, one that she'd learn to live with, but would tear the thin relationship we had to shreds. I'd would spend a few years couch surfing from one aunt to another, to eventually I was financially on my own before I turned 18. In that hour, with no foresight into what would come, all I could do was follow the facts I had. With growing curves and my mother's lack of internal parental guidance system to protect her daughter, Mt. Airy was the safer bet.

I vowed to my younger brother, who was nearing his third birthday, that as soon as I was able, regardless of how old I'd be, as soon as I could take care of him, I would. I re-iterated my earlier intention, the one that I made when my mother first abandoned me, that I would be at least 75% different than all the parental figures in my life. For the sake of survival, it would be crucial. A marked milestone within the memory files of my life, this was the first time I subconsciously redefined what being selfish would mean for me, personally. I knew I had to be selfish enough for myself then, so that there could be an opportunity to help him later. The reward for my deepest regret would be my permission to live.

# Section II:
# Permission to Live

Being bound to the private expectations of our former passions limits our perceived potential. While, surrendering to the expectations of others suffocates us, turning our strength into a shame filled burden. It is in the letting go of these expectations, ours, and theirs, that we revive our hidden desire for freedom and give ourselves the gift of permission to live.

# Letting Go

**4**

Throughout the years to come, I'd experience hurdle, after hurdle, just to jump over and beyond tiny dirt mountains culminated mostly from my own doing. Although I stayed away from drugs and alcohol, with the exception of a Bill Clinton style non-inhale of marijuana moment and those four glasses of sex on the beach with one of my teenage besties that had me vomiting profusely, I went down a different type of self-punishment slope. It would be years before I could move through the guilt I felt for choosing myself over my baby brother. The permission to live that I gave myself came at a cost and the price I'd pay would be internal turmoil. All through high school and into my early adult years, I wrestled with my vacillating attachment issues. I'd fluctuate between avoidant-dismissive behaviors to being anxious and preoccupied. Harboring so much anger and resentment towards my mother and my father, feeling exhausted by my grandmother's mental health illness and gambling addictions, I was furious on the inside, all the time.

For the first year, I'd go visit my youngest brother nearly every weekend. I couldn't bring him back to my grandma's, and I wasn't ready to risk any overnights at my mom's brownstone apartment quite yet, so I'd go and get him for the day and take him to the park most weather conforming days. Old enough to go and visit my younger three siblings without approval from my grandmother now, I wasn't prepared for how I'd feel around them. It was odd, but I was afraid to get too close. I had this nagging feeling that I'd disappoint them too and loose them the way I felt I was losing my baby brother. I'd visit occasionally, but I felt more like a guest then family so often that the visits became farther in between.

At 16, I had three jobs in addition to my school, cheerleading, and cross-country track schedule, so it was becoming harder and harder to travel back in forth. Any boyfriend I'd had at the time, understood that my brother being attached to my hip for most of our dates, which I considered optional social time, was simply non-negotiable. Except for a boy I dated in high school (prior to my husband), you really wouldn't see me outside of the school hallways with a boy, unless my baby brother was with me as well. I didn't make much of a good out-of-school time friend within my female social circle either. My philosophy was, if I don't work, I can't stack, and if I can't stack, I can't save my brother so… most of the regular teenage playtime wasn't on my radar. I won't even waste time telling you how horrible I was to myself about the thought of putting savings away to rent a dress just to go on prom…that's an entirely different bag of unkind self-punishment. In reflection, I can just thank God for few good friends around me that convinced me I deserved to have a night off from work.

I'd be lying if I said I never went to any house parties or jams at the Germantown YMCA. I went to a few, always around my work schedule of course. Laughing and smiling on the outside, tormented with guilt on the inside. So, what did I do? Well, what any other teen would of course, I lashed out. I was incredibly disrespectful with my grandmother every chance I had. My disrespect was direct and would absolutely not be tolerated from my own children so no, I'm not proud of it. My tone was always telling of how angry and enraged I was whenever I had to talk to my grandmother about almost anything. My eye contact was aggressive, like an animal peering through your soul right before it attacked, and my mouth…. oh, my mouth was horrible, primarily with my biological mother, grandmother and when he was around (albeit rarely) my biological father. Imagine for a moment the poster child for talking back and then place my face on the picture.

With all of that said, I still had a few boundaries, mainly the ones built on fear, but I had them. I would never lay a hand on an adult if I planned to keep those hands, and I knew better than to use curse words in front of them. I also knew not to bring people to the house without permission unless I was a 1000% sure no one was home. Of course, during my high school years, that was nearly never since my grandmother was a Registered Nurse that worked the night shift, she was liable to be home all day if she wasn't hitting the casino. At my grandmother's there was really no point of asking for permission because the answer to have anyone over, even female peers to just chill and listen to music with was an emphatically resounding, "no." But like I said earlier, I found other creative and courageous ways to slide down the self-punishment and rebellious teen slope.

I didn't smoke or drink, but I surrounded myself with others who did. Most of my, outside-of-school friends, did a little of anything you could think of. It was my way of riding the line, testing myself, and trying to prove that I was better than her... my mother. In some kind of sick and twisted way, I felt that if I could be around all of this nonsense and not get into anything, that it was confirmation that my mother was purposely choosing to be sick, to stay in her bondage, and that meant I had a choice too. If I could pass my own ridiculous test of exposure to temptation with all my trauma and tough days, that meant my freedom was, in fact, my choice, and I'd win the war against my life. You know, the one society says you are nearly doomed to fail if you come from a highly dysfunctional family with little to no support in a non-inspiring environment? Well, that war could be won if I'd simply past those tests.

If I'm honest, it was the reason I tested those couple of "sex on the beach" drinks. It's also why I tested weed the day I so comically tried to take a few puffs during a cypher with my junior year boyfriend. I truly wanted to inhale correctly but couldn't. I coughed and choked everything up and almost vomited. It's hilarious now, but it was clearly my way of testing my warped version of battleground training — self-limiting belief mixed with a bit of ignorance at its finest.

Was it all in my head? The feeling of needing to vomit. Sure it was... I was subconsciously protecting myself with these psychosomatic reactions, but of course, I didn't know that then. To this day, I can't be around smoke of any kind for too long, and I can barely handle more than two glasses of wine without feeling like I'm losing control. Is it in my head? Sure it is. Do I understand that it's my way of protecting myself, even after years of therapy and being in safe places with safe people? Of course. Do I do it anyway? Yup. My rebellious ways weren't just about my mother and definitely didn't stop with testing myself around drugs and alcohol. My story was littered with a pound of daddy issues too.

My grandmother informed my father about what went down with my mother. Sharing how my mother chose to leave me there with her and my step-grandfather, and that now he would need to go solely through her to arrange visits. I remembered going outside with him, as he leaned against a parked car, we discussed how I felt betrayed by my mother and in my own 9-year words, how disappointed I was. My father was comforting. He mirrored my disappointment through his eyes and body language as he assured me that everything would be absolutely fine.

I never told him about the happenings with my step-grandfather, just that I didn't like him, and how he didn't treat me like his grandson, my cousin that was born from his biological daughter, my mother's younger sister. I had already been told the stories about how my grandfather pulled a gun out on my father years earlier. According to my grandmother, it was because my father had put his hands on my mother, so my step-grandfather went four blocks around the corner to Elaine Street to leave an impression. My grandmother doted that it was because my step-grandfather wasn't going to allow anyone to hurt one of his kids. Even at a young age, I knew that was pure B.S. It was more like, he didn't anyone damaging his property accept him... Because I knew the history and was old enough to understand that telling my father would lead to one of them in jail and the other in a grave, I buried my truth and my trauma. I wasn't willing to have my father pulled away from me because of my pain. I felt like it's mine, so I needed to handle it on my own.

I shared superficial issues like how he would send me to the corner store to get a dollar's worth of 10 cent twin popsicles and give my cousin one but tell me that I couldn't have one because I looked at him funny. He would suggest my looks were disrespectful. I'd told my father about how he would call me stupid a lot and tell me that I couldn't look at him in his eyes because it was disrespectful, but that I'd do it anyway. I didn't have the verbiage or fully understand it at the time, but I knew there was power in my stare. I made him uncomfortable, and that made me feel somehow like I was equalizing the playing field for what he would do to me on nights when he would come get me out of my bed. In addition to being afraid to lose my father to some sort of life sentence or death, I held back descriptions of those nights because I thought he'd look at me like I was less, and not see me as his little girl anymore. Instead I stayed within the part of the share that wouldn't make him ask any questions that would lead him to the truth. It was the result of my earlier script to take care of the needs of others first.

We stood outside the house that day for what felt like hours but may have only been minutes. I felt supported for the first time that I could think of, by my father that day. About 4-6 months later, my father told me on one of his visits that my stepmom was also doing drugs and they were having a hard time. He didn't tell me the type of drug, nor what having a hard time meant exactly, but I imagined that my two other siblings were going through something similar to what I was, though they were much younger and may not have understood as much at that point. I felt sad for my dad. I wanted to help him. In my head, I could heal him with a hug. It's all I could give at nearly ten years old, and to this day, it's one of my favorite ways to transfer my compassion and positive energy with others.

My issues with my father didn't come during that outdoor conversation. They didn't come when he shared the unfortunate news about my stepmom. They didn't even come after the countless times, I'd sit, shivering in the cold, hard, cement steps outside of the redbrick rowhome, waiting patiently for hours for him to come pick me up for one of our visits, that he'd conveniently forget about. None of those things were enough to pull back or push him away. My daddy issues showed up about six months after our outdoor heart-to-heart when my father showed up at my grandmother's house high. He too had joined in on the 80's epidemic of crack cocaine, and I was now void of being able to depend on any of the blood relative adult figures in my life. Within six months of each other, back to back, there was literally no adult family member safe enough to rely on or trust. In my mind, they were all giving up on me.

As a kid, I didn't understand their addiction was pre-empted by their need to relieve their dysphoria, a pro-longed dissatisfaction with life. I definitely didn't understand the impending cycle to achieve the result of their first high. An endless loop of chasing the 1st experience of increased dopamine and opioid peptide activity in their brain's reward circuits, would become a two-fold curse to either chase it or be burdened to fight and flee from a disease that would haunt them every second of every day.

What I could see was the choice they were making to partake in something besides protecting and guiding me. I felt like I wasn't good enough to stay whole for, so they were choosing to succumb to something they felt was more important. Out of everyone, I distanced myself from my father the most after that night. He wasn't just the final betrayal, he was literally, the last hope standing and the first expectation of being someone that I could ever lean on that I'd need to let go so I could move forward.

## Dirty Talk & Disillusions

By the time I hit high school in the early '90s, I had already experienced nearly every violation you could think of. I had also felt the universe's pull on my gift, and I pushed back with an unwavering acknowledgment that I didn't want the burden of empathic abilities and exhortation. After you've been told more than 100 times that you'd turn out to be just like the person who'd abandoned you, who chose to numb their pain and chase a high instead of fighting for or at least with you, these expectations become something you lean in on and live down to, because truly, what else is there.

The reality is I knew better. On a spiritual level, I felt that there was more. But he pushes and pulls off what was scripted against what I tried to re-write for myself felt overtaxing at times. There were days when I could live into my new reality, the persona I took on was of an extraverted, super bubbly, happy go lucky, hugger! It was who I wanted to be, my illustration of what someone who was 75% opposite of my family members would look like. During those contrived happy go lucky moments, it really didn't bother me when other people were annoyed at how happy I seemed. I was always smiling, connected to the needs of others. A complete joiner! I signed up for all the things my grandmother told me I couldn't, cheerleading, cross-country, and even the informal virgin's club a few friends and I created to separate ourselves from the other, well...nonvirgins of our high school.

I held a fairly decent GPA and worked three jobs throughout high school, somehow still making room for relationships. At least superficially. But everything about this persona was my attempt at creating a new reality. A bit of my dream state worked out loud. Like all dreams, waking interruptions in the form of reality glitches would often occur. Instead of trying to smother them, I incorporated them. My reality was that I wasn't a virgin in the physical sense. But since I had never consented to any of those violations that stole what I didn't fully understand was sacred, I enveloped myself in a bit of a hypocritical bubble, a pseudo haven from the glitches of my awaken state.

I found myself easily sliding into controversial and inappropriate conversations. I'd use my profound sense of sarcasm to veil the truth that I hoped no one would sense. If one of my classmates said something even close to cheeky, like, "Hey, come here for a sec," I'd lean in and say, "oh, so you want me to *cum* here, hah?" and start laughing. Totally inappropriate, unnecessarily dirty, and ridiculous, I know. But it was what I did to cope with the duality of feelings I had going on inside between head and my heart, frozen in a locked box of traumatic memories filled to the brim with powerlessness, fear, and lack of control. It didn't matter that I wasn't sexually active, had barely had more than a consensual kiss, and wasn't interested in doing anything beyond that. No one needed to know that I was petrified of the very thing I spoke so openly about. I didn't want to be as an oversexualized girl, so I'd play everything down with humor and play my innocence up with silly or naïve facial expressions that confused my peers, just enough to avoid any permanent labels. The displayed naivety and gullibility was simply armor and an unconscious example of my early brilliance, completely unbalanced.

I'd understand later in life, that it was an expression of the internal struggle to embrace all that was good and positive about my sensuality and the fight to avoid anything that would make me appear as a weaker vessel in a power play for sexual dominance. I always needed to be in control, even if that meant taking the reins in a way that appeared as if I was living down to the expectation that I'd be just like what my mother was seen. A price I was willing to pay in order to secretly create a reality I could live up to...

To my surprise, this exhibited duality would come at a much higher toll than I'd emotionally prepared for. Between my afterschool job at Roy Rogers in Cheltenham, babysitting, and working at the local Wadsworth Pizzeria as a closer (coming in the house between 1 a.m. to 3 a.m. on school nights), cheerleading practice, cross country races, and sneaking to meet my boyfriend every other week to chill, I got yelled at quite a bit. I received more than my share of beat-downs but wasn't broken from them. I didn't know how, nor did I want to learn how to be quiet. I didn't need to curse or raise my hand, I merely never refrained from saying what was on my mind, the epitome of a disrespectful teenager to anyone who gave the slightest hint of threatening posture, tone, or demean-

or towards me. To all others, I was a squeaky-voiced angel who smiled incessantly.

## What Will Be Will Be

The boy I allowed myself to date freshman year, wasn't my first choice, but I didn't feel ready for the one I had an instinctual connection with at first sight. Instead, I opted to bury my private crush below the depths of my dreams, knowing that the boy I liked the most wouldn't be able to handle any of the wacky I was carrying in those days. I embraced my first sight crush in my energy space as a friend, one I'd call brother for now as I knew in my gut, he'd one day become my husband. When I tell you, my intuitive gifts were potent, I mean they were off the charts. But more on that later.

In the interim, the first high school boy I dated was opposite of anything that I would normally be interested in, but we connected through unspoken pain and tons of laughter. There were broken pieces scattered around him, and I couldn't resist the need to fix what I could sense needed repair. An adopted multicultural kid, well over 6' tall, broad shoulders, chocolate, and filled with a rage that only abuse could create. He wasn't the first person in my life I'd unconsciously stay too long in a relationship with simply because I felt the need to rescue him from himself. Today, we'd all recognize this as a vicarious way to save myself. There was no abuse, yet, it was completely unhealthy.

Most of my high school, I barely stretched out to 4' 9", weighed 115lbs on a bloated day, had smooth skin, sandy brown hair with natural reddish blonde highlights, hazel eyes, and a thin athletes body that I kept covered in piece together hand-me downs. At the beginning of our relationship, I knew that I was a bit of a trophy girlfriend for him. I was far from the most popular, nor the most stylish, and wasn't what the boys would consider a "10," but I wasn't low on self-esteem which was its own potent magnet of attraction. A naturally cute chick that didn't need to do the extra to own a sense of my beauty with a dash of unbothered, created a recipe of unconventional swagger. I didn't understand my power or prowess back then. But I had a sense of my awkward and quirky humor, wasn't arrogant, illuminated a slightly rebellious spirit, and could hold my own in conversation and in the street, if necessary. Something many of my male peers found intoxicating. Looking back, it was in my best interest that I ignored 99% of the love-drunk boys that tried to slip into my broken vessel.

I recognized at an early age that there would be passes given to me, simply for being a light-skinned girl. It was an unearned privilege that I knew was inherently wrong and understood the conspiratorial history of it from a young age. Because of the fairness of my skin, people overlooked some obvious flaws in my character, dismissed red flags that were easily detected in the duality displays noted above, and complimented me for average things that my more melanated sisters would be overlooked for. Colorism is a thing and it exist in and outside of the black and brown communities. Now that it's been stated and perhaps just reaffirmed, you have an obligation to be aware and not be a part of the problem... As a teenager, I was aware that this was an attraction point for my first high school boyfriend, and even then, it bothered me. But I was conflicted. Everyone has characteristics they prefer or better stated, "types." Was it bad that his type at the time was light skinned? Should I be ashamed of being light skinned because others might wrongly prefer or disapprove of my skin without giving me an opportunity to show them who I was as a human? These questions would come up for repeatedly until I understood the script that formulated them, which won't be for a few more years from now. Let's mark this as a to be continued area of self-discovery shall we...

Back to my earlier point, there was nothing especially significant about much of our relationship in the first year. We got to know each other as much as either of us would allow ourselves to do. Our reciprocal exchange was in the hidings of plain sight that we were able to do with one another. He was able to hide his pain in humor, just as I did, and we both were able to do what we did well, not deal with whatever really needed to be dealt with. He made me laugh from my core, a natural comedian that really wasn't trying to be funny, but it was his duality. If he didn't have you laughing, you were typically trying to keep him from crushing in a car with his bare fist or hope you could talk him out of fighting.

His anger never frightened me. I had a bit of delusional confidence inside, and it told me that he was a danger only to those that would get in his way at the wrong time. That would never be me, so I focused on fixing. Being his encouragement, empowering him to make better choices, to handle his adopted mother's bouts of rage differently, and contain his fears. As our relationship moved deeper, he could make me smile within seconds of looking at me, and I appreciated the way he made me feel. His gaze was refreshing, safe, non-lustful, and full. I didn't know at the time, that I should never set out to complete anyone, that we should come to each other already complete, but again, I'm 14 here people... In those days, the look of fulfillment felt good, it didn't need to be right. Honestly, I wasn't rushing towards right, I simply needed about 75% different.

For the first year and a half of my relationship with the first high school boyfriend, we were both virgins, talked on the phone more than we shared space outside of school hallways and classrooms, and occasionally chilled at his mom's house when she worked a late shift on one of the rare evenings I didn't have one of my 3 jobs to work. We broke up during the summer between freshmen and sophomore year because, selfishly, while I was staying with my mom in South Philly the first few years of high school, I had a separate existence outside of school. Summertime offered a sense of freedom and choice. I could float through neighborhoods and avoid being hugged up with someone who expected all my outside of school/work time. Since we didn't have the bridge of a daily class schedule to force us to share our space, I was able to build a towering wall around me that I named boundary. Truth is, I was a bit emotionally bulimic. I would binge on empowering, listening, and fixing and then vomit his attention and need for closeness on weekends, most school holidays, and throughout the summer by pulling up my tower.

It's an odd thing to admit, but when we got back together in the first few weeks of our 10th-grade year, it was literally because he kept asking. The peers in our too-small school kept highlighting how he was such a good guy and how heartbroken he appeared. Key root word, *broken*. I fix things, I don't break them, is what I thought. So, I agreed to try it again. Since I'm on a role with admitting my life's faults and youthful overly self-important moments, I might as well share that I was also tired of being one of the last few virgins in my school. It's a nerdy thing to say, but it was my truth. I was a part of a small private virgins' club, and there were like three of us left by this sophomore year (give or take). My first consensual sexual experience wasn't because of hormones, or attraction, lust, anticipated pleasure nor pressure. I had sex because I was looking for a sense of control. I wanted to do something on my own terms and not give anyone else permission to lead that moment for me.

Less than two weeks after moving out of the South Philly brownstone and feeling the regret of having to leave behind my baby brother, I was emotionally drained. I was tired of the 24/7 torment I caused myself over leaving him. I was tired of the failed problem-solving attempts to discover how I could save him and myself simultaneously. I was even tired of not knowing what it felt like to have sex with someone that I invited to touch me. I took control, loss my consensual virginity in less than one-minute of passionless sex and broke out in a nearly uncontrollable rage when I saw that my boyfriend took the condom off to, as he would so ignorantly say "feel me more." That was my lightbulb moment, and the end of my need to fix him. If only I had let go completely of trying to fix people in general that day as well, life would've been so much easier.

About a month later, I went in a little early to my volunteer shift at Planned Parenthood as a Teen Sex counselor no less and found out that I was pregnant. As you can see, my life was and is filled with juxtapositions. So now, at 15, living back in the redbrick home in Mt. Airy, safe from everything except the sporadic bouts of anger and incoherent ramblings of my grandmother who hadn't been diagnosed with an undisclosed mental health illness, I'm a walking statistic. Pregnant, high school sophomore — carrying a child from another broken child who I tolerate but don't have any deep feelings for, and clearly neither of us are in any kind of position to take care of another human. I was tormented over the reality that I had just walked into a version of my mother's and grandmother's life. My anguish went on for about three weeks before my body miscarried and dismissed the possibility of having to drop out of high school to be a mother.

You might expect me to say that I was horrified, or at least upset. I wasn't. I was thankful that my first invited experience, my first high school boyfriend, and first recognized unhealthy relationship and I could move on without ties for the next 18+ years. I was as you can imagine, irritated with him and disgusted with myself for wasting my consent on him. A nice guy, just immature, covered in emotional hurt and no match for me. This is what happens when you deal with a girl with unprocessed trauma, baggage, anger, three generations of damage, and enough pain to fill a football stadium. Attachment, or lack thereof in my case, is most certainly a core issue...

## Reflect & Celebrate
### *Lessons Learned*

Your freedom is indeed your choice, so choose you! But this freedom cost. The minimum deposit requires you to dig up your buried pain, forgive yourself for the hurt you caused yourself and others, and **let go** of your need to fix everyone but yourself. In an ideal world, you should process and maintain accountability to your self-love with a trusted, preferably professionally trained person who can help you understand that it's not a burden your soul should bear alone.

As you get stronger, being able to *give* and **receive** something as small as a gentle, authentic, hug may not accountability heal you, but the increase in oxytocin it releases reduces blood pressure and the stress hormone norepinephrine.

In its simplest form, real hugs really help.

# Change Agents-
## Good, Bad, and
## Crucial

**5**

W e've all had them, and with every breath of life we each receive, there's a new opportunity to encounter another as we become one for others. Change agents. They come in all shapes, sizes, ethnicities, and cultural backgrounds. Some bring with them tons of good; some bring too much bad, and others are simply crucial factors and bring a little of both to us along our journey. What is most significantly equal for all of them, is that they will undoubtedly open a wedge of space between what you thought you knew of yourself and what you will become. Often these agents of change will fool you into thinking they are the designers of that space, when, the truth is it always existed.

Each change agent, whether you attracted them, or they were divinely appointed to you, had and has a purpose. The allowing that occurs when they enter into your physical reality is always *for you* to see the opportunity that lives inside a previously hidden wedge of space, one where you get to choose what is possible as you develop into your greatest being. My mother, father, siblings, grandmother, aunts, two uncles, stepmom, mom-in love, godparents, my soul's half (my husband), and yes, even my abusers were what I now recognize as **crucial** change agents in my life. Without them and the experiences they brought with them that opened me to the numerous wedges of space our encounters revealed, are undeniably *why* I am. But from here, let me take you back a few decades to just a few interconnected change agents that would impact my life in the most subtle yet profound ways.

In the early '90s, there were quite a few agents of change attracted *(and)* appointed to my reality. Throughout my high-school experience, most of the change agents I attracted were animated mirrors of my insecurities wrapped in flesh. Quick to help, give, and fix as an unconscious means to bury the pain of quietly kept secrets, I smiled so much I annoyed most and befriended those who were magnets to my outwardly cheery disposition. It wouldn't be long before game recognized game, and the ones who were appointed in my life would stand above the fray of attracted imposters who posed as friends or even called themselves sisters. An endearing phrase I've learned to extend extremely sparingly as an adult. But as a child, I did childish things and hence had to grow through the pain of lessons that would bring out an inner strength I didn't know existed.

The first notable lesson would be born from the ashes of a sistership that simply flamed out because neither of us cared enough to keep the fire going. We were young, lived within blocks of each other, shared the same nickname, and for a short while, went to the same school — a recipe for relatability and good old young girl fun. There were no major incidents or issues, we were just slowly growing apart. Especially once she transferred to Girls High, a school that would require her to simply take a different bus route and lead to us taking different paths in life. Don't get me wrong, she's an incredible person, successful, and seems to be enjoying life based on what I've seen on Facebook (if you can go by that), but are commonalities dissipated when our schedules stopped overlapping. Prior to that, this friend, who I'll call Rita, introduced me to a boy who led me to a girl that would change my life.

Rita was dating a peculiar boy just a few years older than her, from her grandmother's neighborhood. Her parents weren't too keen on her being in that neighborhood without supervision or at least with a trusted friend who they thought she'd stay out of trouble with. Since I had that good old painted smiled thing working for me, her parents thought I was a sweet and mostly innocent friend, so they encouraged us to hang out together. I was a good cover story if Rita was late getting home or didn't answer her parent's page right away. If she said she was with me, picking up my baby brother or something of the like, they were less likely to snap and hand out grounding punishments. Rita started to really get into this older boy, we'll call him Devon, and she wanted to spend more time with him, so she needed me to become a better cover story than just someone she said she was with, she wanted me to actually be there.

Rita introduced me to Devon's best friend, Antonio. He was also peculiar, in a different way than Rita's Devon, but just my kind of interesting. A young Italian, Native American mixed with African American, he had a familiar cuteness to him. I just couldn't put my fingers on it at the time. Antonio was smart, funny, and well known in his neighborhood. It was refreshing to be around someone who seems to just know people without acting like he wanted to show off and be known. Now this relationship with Antonio and I would grow into my first hot and heavy relationship, and there would be lots of teenage drama, but only a few moments are noteworthy. Those moments wouldn't occur until after Rita and Devon broke up. Their fling was typical-teenage brief, and I'm sure if you asked her today, she'd barely have any memories beyond the fact that he was mostly a jerk to her, and she was glad it ended when it did.

But here I am, still connected to Devon through Antonio now that we're an item. Those two are practically brothers, so I'm privy to anyone new Devon's dating. Hence, the introduction to the girl. Devon's next serious lover would become one of my best friends. Devina Cruz. One of seven children, this Afro-Latina, was a force to reckon with. She wore her pain on her sleeve, and it was covered in the same colored paint I wore. There was no question, we had body trauma kinship and were sisters bred from the grains of generational secrets never told outside of sacred spaces. Devina could make bad things look good without convincing you. There were days when Devon would get on her last good nerves, and she'd call me up and say, come over so I can do your hair. Now, if you know me, you know I've never been into nor good with my hair. Simple wraps or ponytails were my go-to, so I didn't mind someone else dealing with my tresses when I clearly refused to. I'd go to Devon's house, where Devina was staying at the time, she'd do my hair and then say, let's go meet up with my cousins in North (North Philly). I could see it in her eyes and feel in the air that she didn't just want to go say hi, but the bad didn't settle as bad when she'd hint towards it. It just seemed like the next step.

Like I mentioned before, there were only two times in my life I ever tested myself with drinking alcohol to a threshold, and my trip with Devina to see her cousins was the first. I was 15 (looking like I was 12), in a bar, in north Philly, and no one asked any questions. Devina, just like Antonio, seemed to know everyone, and everyone knew her, so there were no questions. We were fearless, reckless, and thankfully covered by angels. I can't imagine the heart attack I'd have if my daughter did even an eighth of what I did during my friendship with her. Divinely appointed, Devina was crucial for my journey. Along with the bad that she made easy, she brought great things to my awareness. I just had to watch, listen, and respond from my intuition. It would be through our friendship that I would begin to pay attention to the center of my gut (and) respond with it.

Devina and Devon's relationship was volatile. Often, violent outbursts would break out from what began as a small disagreement over something as menial as who left water in the bathroom floor after a shower. Normal things that most young couples might bicker over. But there bickering would lead to things getting broken. Devina was a fighter and reminded me a lot of my mom. She felt like as long as she gave as good as she got, then she wasn't being abused, it was just a squabble that they'd recover from after a few hours. I told her at least two dozen times that she needed to be out of the relationship and got to the point that I didn't want to be around either of them. It was hard to look at Devon without wanting to punch him in the throat. Antonio made so many excuses for him that it caused our already shaky relationship to splinter into two planes. Antonio started to smoke more weed and displayed more paranoid accusatory behavior. I was over it and broke up with him.

But my dear friend Devina had other plans for us. She knew me well enough to know that I wasn't for the b.s, but also knew that me leaving Antonio could mean that our bond could wither simply because we wouldn't have the conveniences of being around each other as much. I wouldn't have agreed with her at the time, but the truth is, she would've been correct. When you're young, most of your friendships are solidified by the common things you share, primarily time. The less you have with each other, the more likely you become the person they used to know... Neither of us wanted to become a memory for the other, our friendship mattered, until it was fractured.

Devina was pressured into talking me into coming over to her and Devon's spot (where they shared the basement of his mother's house), so Antonio could try to win me back. Her good intention was to go along with the plan so that everything could get back to normal, and we would all be the four amigos again. She called me up, telling me she needed help with something and asked me to come over. It wasn't often that Devina asked for help, but when she did, I always came through. Loyal. To a fault. When I got there, I realized it was a set up for Antonio and me to talk. But it quickly turned into a discovery of the depths of my rage. Antonio was high as a kite, the whites of his eyes were bloodshot red from drinking, and his words were slurred. All I kept thinking was why Devina would think we'd be able to get back together and what makes her think we aren't fighting when this is over! The entire scene was something out of a bad movie.

Devina and Devon went upstairs to give me and Antonio time to speak privately. I told them both there was no need because we didn't need to talk. They both chuckled a bit as if I wasn't serious and walked away. Antonio and I were alone for less than 10-15 minutes before I blacked out in a fit of rage. What I can tell you is that I remember Antonio didn't just want to talk. He became more aggressive when I tried to leave the house and tried to rape me. I remember picking up a gold running trophy, one of many that Devon's sisters had on the shelves of his mothers' home and cracking Antonio over the head with it. I remember the screams, his, and Devon and Devina trying to pull me off Antonio. There was blood everywhere, and I just kept saying to Devina, "why would you do that," over and over again.

Devina's good intentions nearly cost me a murder case. You'd think I was angry with her; I wasn't. I was disappointed that she didn't realize how dangerous it would be to have me in that type of situation. We had so much in common, yet at that moment, I realize just how completely different we were. Devina would stay in a space that gave her no oxygen, and I would risk my future to escape it. That moment was the catalyst. I pulled all the way away and was finally able to see the wedge that Devina's appointment in my life brought me to. The day she called to ask for my help, I felt the pull in my gut that said no, and I ignored it. The wedge of space that moment showed me was to pay attention and respond accordingly.

My relationship with Devina was fractured. Like my mothers, I loved her and wanted the best for her, but I needed to create boundaries for myself that would keep me from defaulting into the rescuer. The reality is the drama triangle that occurs when you try to save or rescue someone, and it leads you into being the one that's resented and pushed away. A slow lesson, one that would be repeated in my life a few times before I really received it permanently, but my relationship with Devina was the first friendship, where I'd pause to admit that backing up was the best action and one that may have saved my life more than once.

## The Deepest Cut

August 1998, a few years after my soul's half and I had graduated high-school, started undergraduate, and blessed the earth with our firstborn son, who was now two-years old, I'd get a call from Devina's sister that would bring me to my knees. Devina and her son, who was just a few months older than my son, were murdered in a triple murder suicide by Devon. Devina had left him again, one of the many times they'd broken up, and she'd leave to go to her mother's house with their son for respite before he'd woo her back into his layer. He went over to convince her to go home with him again, and she refused and resisted. Devina's sister found her holding her baby boy, cradling him from the death sentence his own father administered by slashing his throat. Devina had protection wounds all over her arms, face, and back, trying to protect her son, and would die doing so. Devon stabbed himself in the heart and was found on top of both bodies.

A piece of my spirit was buried with Devina and Devon's first child and only child. Going to the funeral, I could barely speak. There was a lump in my throat so big I am sure you'd thought I had a tumor protruding from my neck. I ached in every part of my body, down to my toes. The thought that I could've had one more conversation helped in any way to protect her, convinced her to leave and never open the door for him again, played over and over in my head like a broken record player. One should never see a toddler in a casket, covered in makeup to cover knife wounds or any other form of injury from their parent, ever. It's not the natural order of things, and no one can convince me that it is. As a trauma specialist, I'd come across many similar catastrophes, and no, it never gets easier, but the ones that are the most difficult to bear, are the ones that you felt you could've prevented. No matter how wrong or disillusioned you might be about that possibility, the feeling cuts deep into your spirit and leaves an unshakeable imprint that never goes away.

# Posturing to Pass for Average

## 6

Throughout my youth, most of the expectations that tethered me were those set by the adults in my life. They were few, contradictory, and mostly negative, but they were my baseline. I'd hear, "don't be like your mother," "you're going to be just like your mother," "your stupid," all the way to "I'm sure you'll work it out." My aims weren't high; they were dreamy and well above the realm of the world, I walked in daily. As a young child, I dreamed of being a pediatrician with a psychology office on the side of my rather large home. Somehow, I knew I'd be able to save children and figure out what was wrong with their parents at the same time. As I got older, the dream got fuzzier and a bit contorted along the way. But as I moved through the days, I found myself playing small, hiding my dreams from most, and only sharing superficial layers of myself, if anything at all. It was if I wanted them to think I was more normal than I was, and the only way I knew to do that was to posture so I could pass for an average girl. In my spirit, I knew I was quite a bit more than normal, much more on the unusual/awkward/special spice side of life and most of the people I attracted couldn't handle what I mirrored in them just as much as I didn't want to admit that I attracted inverted versions of myself towards me.

Life shifted as I leaned in more to my curiosities with boldness and the courage to be rejected. Adopting the idea that my brother-like friend, who I'd had a secret affinity for since I first laid eyes on him four years prior, would lead to a surprising reward. There were so many reasons that I justified and created in my head for not leaning into what it would feel like to talk to him on the level of boyfriend to girlfriend until the day I stepped up into the feeling. We were standing at a bus stop together, and I literally squared up my shoulders, stood right in front of him in his personal space, and asked him if he'd be my jump off! He looked at me deeply and said, "Yes!" That's the entire love story. The one we unapologetically share with other couples when they ask, how did you move from friends to lovers at such a young age. Hah! The truth is, we were 17 years old, immature, and both extremely direct. Our "love story" began with my request that he'd be my sex partner. How romantic, I know. Yet, here we are, over 25 years later, still friends, lovers, and now, partners on a deeper level than where we began.

Sounds like a hood fairytale, but our relationship was far from fairy anything. Dean, my soul's half, and I had to grow up together, and that meant growing through our own painful lessons as entangled to ourselves in each other's process. It was often messy, frustrating, and at times, overwhelming. Now there are decades of stories that I simply won't share, not because it's private (clearly, I've been more than a little open until this point), but those moments are more integral to his memoir than my own. What I can do is walk you through a few of the most impactful moments I experienced and were crucial elements for the personal transformation I own, mine. For his, is just that, his.

Dean was instrumental in my process. He was like a circus mirror, reflecting multiple reflections of me, yet none of them looked identical to the one that I would see in a normal mirror. He challenged me to be better, dig deeper, and not accept what was in front of me as what I deserved. If you ask him today, he'll tell you half-jokingly that he saved me from me. We both chuckled at that whenever he says it; then I reverberate that I saved him right back, only I'm not joking. Now I know I told you that no one could *truly* save anyone else because it creates a drama triangle ending in resentment. That's 1000% true. We also did, in fact, save each other, and we also resented each other for it. Over time, we were able to release each other from the narrative we created and locked ourselves into. More on that later.

Dean, a mocha brown, 5'10, black man who could pass for quite a few different nationalities depending on the light you looked at him under, was completely opposite of me in nearly every way you could imagine. He was quiet, vigilant, and moved about with an air stealth swiftness. I was loud, negligent when it came to observing most things unless they were safety related, and moved about, well, loudly. But our chemistry was undeniable. To say I was attracted to him is an understatement. Dean's body was incredible, but it was his mind that pulled me in deep. Of course, we have words for that now, and I understand that I'm what you'd call a sapiosexual (attracted to intelligence). He could literally talk about air, and it would make me moist. A wordsmith, creative, and lyricist with a touch of mystery and a dash of OCD. The first time we made love, he literally took time to fold up each piece of his clothing and place it in a neat stack while I laid there completely naked. I contemplated for a second if this was going to be a deal breaker, thinking, "is he seriously taking his time getting to all this goodness, wasting time folding clothes?" Those thoughts quickly dissipated when he showed me what he was working with. I should've known he was going to be my baby daddy when his sex-drive literally wore me out over 3-hours in and I had to ask for breaks to catch my breath. There was no question, he was made for me, and my lack of self-love coupled with our youthful immaturity nearly ended our love story before it truly took roots.

A little perspective here. The first few years of our love song in the making, Dean and I were grappling with more unprocessed grief than agreement. The summer after high-school graduation, before we'd both go on to college, we were tested with a little distance. I spent the summer at my aunt and uncles in New Jersey, babysitting their first son while they worked and making a few dollars for school, or at least that was the plan. In the '90s, we didn't all have long-distance included cell phone plans, you'd have to pay for those conversations when the bill came in. We sat on the phone for hours, sometimes talking, often, quietly lingering inside each other's energy. There was never any pressure to force conversation, nor were we rushing to unplug from each other. We could simply be. Until that dang on phone bill came to my aunt's house for over $900... She was never one to play games or pacify my nonsense, so I worked that summer in exchange for verbal cuddles with my boo. Still, it was worth it. Teenager's need for instant gratification and lack of patients typically shorten the length of long-distance relationships. For us, it solidified our bond, and our love was strengthened that summer. As we moved towards our respective freshman years, his at Temple University, Communications Major and mine at Drexel University,

Pre-Med with a Psychology, Sociology, and Anthropology Majors (because I've always been ridiculous), our destiny locked in on a level neither of us was prepared.

## Secret Recovery

Fall '95, just a few weeks into my freshman semester, Dean had a near death accident at school, which led to him temporarily losing sight in his right-eye and losing fingers on his right hand. While he was in the hospital, I found out I was 16 weeks pregnant with not one, not two, but three babies. It was a bittersweet moment. Dean was in so much pain, we all feared for him, and here I was pregnant with his child. In true Naketa fashion, I denied the pain I felt, by digging into what I could control, my schedule. I wanted him to stay focused on his full recovery and not be caught in any mental drama, so I started my prenatal care, went to class, work, and to back to the hospital every day. My occasional headaches turned into a never-ending ache from all the tension and pressure. I didn't realize I was developing prenatal hypertension until it was too late. A little over a month later, a little after midnight on a cold Tuesday morning, I'd deliver 22-week old stillborn babies. I hadn't really processed the fact that I was pregnant with multiples and had only thought of one name prior to the delivery, so we'd forever call them *Lakim and the twins.*

Dean was still in recovery, and I was alone. I didn't want to hold them, and I didn't want to know what their gender was. I simply wanted to escape my body and my mind. I buried a piece of my spirit that night, tucked it right under the graveyard of bones filled with markers engraved with my trauma. Dean and I would both be in physical and emotional recovery after that night, but only one of us would allow support during that time. My recovery would be kept secret, not because he asked, but because I thought he needed it, and I refused to believe I deserved it. I convinced myself I simply didn't have time to grieve or deal with the rush of competing emotions. I knew this felt completely different than my first miscarriage and it was clearly more involved. These extremely small beings were tiny children, who's toes, and fingers were easily distinguishable. They were the most potent shade of red I'd ever seen in my life, and I felt a sense of sorrow I'd never experienced before. All that said, I had to tether myself to what my reality was, and clearly, it did not include sharing in their lives, so I had no right to be sad about it. At least that's what I told myself whenever I needed to push the lump of emotion back down my throat.

As Dean recovered physically, he gravitated to me in a new way. We created a universe that included just the two of us. As soon as he could move around, he started coming to my dorm at Calhoun Hall as often as he could.

His parents weren't happy about it, and they knew he needed to rest. They also knew their son. He needed a semblance of normalcy and belonging just as much as I did. We got so lost in other at times that my roommate, who was also an early childhood friend, would get pissed. I didn't get it at the time, but I guess it was a little bit more than annoying to feel like she shared her room with a couple when that's not what she signed up for. Dean was at my dorm so much the security guards and front desk reception gave him head nods as he came in and barely checked his I.D. That wasn't the making of a respectful roommate situation, but it was a set up for us to be in trouble again...

By the middle of the third term of my freshman year at Drexel, I had a private room in the dorm. My roommate and I had a major falling out. Both of us were beyond immature, said extremely hurtful things to each other, and ended up as two fearlessly scrappy Philly girls would, in a physical fight that could've gotten both of us thrown out of school permanently. Fortunately, neither of us was expelled, and we were offered the opportunity for one of us to just move to a recently vacant room on another floor. Without hesitation, I moved out and up to the sixth floor. You'd think that it would be in the new privacy that would lead us into young love trouble, but you'd be mistaken. I was already more than three months pregnant before I moved. Yes, I know...Naketa, what were you and Dean thinking! Trust me when I tell you, we were NOT trying to get pregnant, and all our future children were created partially because it was God's plan and partially because my boyfriend/future husband had super sperm....

## My Next Chapter - Shaking the Shame

After the initial shock that we were going to be parents, Dean's parents both accepted it in their own way. His mom (my mother-in-love, who I only refer to as mommy from here on out) would be encouraging and talk to us about staying focused on doing right by ourselves, each other, and this child we'd agreed to bring into the world. Never one to mince her words, mommy, would check us on everything from what I chose to eat to what ob-gyn doctor I would go to for good prenatal care. She could care less how I felt about anything that didn't seem like what she felt was best for her grandchild, and to be honest, she was usually right. Dean's father was less encouraging and more logistical. He had a pretty direct conversation with him about how we were going to take care of the child financially. Although he knew I worked multiple jobs while I was in school, he knew they were all minimum wage part-time positions that weren't going to cut it with the new responsibility we had coming our way. After their less than fuzzy-hearted discussion, Dean told me he was dropping out of his Communications program at Temple to concentrate on work for our family. He convinced me that he'd go back after I graduated, mostly because he knew that's what I needed to here, so I'd drop the issue and not talk him out of what he felt was the best choice.

My grandmother and two maternal aunts who raised me and who's couched I'd surfed in my earlier teenage years were less than encouraging, and none of them were supportive. To sum it up, my grandmother asked me, "what kind of father Dean could be as dark [skinned] as he is" ... then told me we needed to get married if we were having a baby. In her eyes, it was the only option, and it didn't matter that I didn't want to rush into a marriage. Beyond the idiocy of her in-group racism and colorist views, which were ridiculous on multiple levels, including the fact that my grandfather and all the men in her life were dark-skinned... I brought up to her that my parents did that, and they were unhappy and divorced by the time I was three-years-old. She kindly retorted, "so, at least you weren't born out of wedlock..." The juxtapositions that existed in my family were from a bad episode of the x-files. Both of my aunts were hard-hitting and left their imprints after our conversations. They both loved me, and neither of them knew how to talk to me, let alone empower me. What I got, in turn, was a verbal beratement about my life choices that led me to end both calls with the beginning of years of emotional and physical distance that would begin between us.

Over the next few years, Dean and I would become parents to a healthy, beautiful, creative baby boy. We would move at least three times while I maintained multiple jobs, co-op internships, and my standing on Drexel's Dean's list. He'd unintentionally become an at-home father since the cost of even subsidized daycare was more expensive than we could afford. We would also avoid talking about my nightmares, the flashes of abuse I endured that impacted our intimacy at every level, or the fact that my hypervigilance and mood swings were off the charts. Neither of us realized that living together would be challenged on an incomprehensible level when we agreed to take over my grandmother's mortgage at the small red-brick house in Mt. Airy.

Up until this point, I had only shared headlines with him about the abuse I had endured as a child. It didn't occur to me that giving birth to a child, nor raising him in the very home where the abuse occurred could trigger unwanted memories to arise. There were constant reminders literally crawling out of the walls, the same paneling, and carpet that I stared at when I would count in my head as a way to disappear from the pain and icky, sticky, yuckiness that I felt as a child was staring back at me when Dean, my friend, and lover would try to make me laugh or create a romantic moment. The screams in my head were noisier than his love, and the pain of my trauma began to harden my spirit. I'd walk away from Dean and go start working on a paper that wasn't due yet or look at our bank statement balances and try to think of how many more hours I could put in to help catch up with bills. All of these tasks would create an irresistible pressure; the stress it created was familiar and calming, like medicine; it dulled my pain.

This was a new girl he was meeting, one so very different than the one he fell in love with, and there was nothing I could do to keep him from her introduction. The 21 months we lived in the small redbrick house in Mt. Airy was by far the most damaging on our relationship and we're just getting started. We tried to create new memories to trump the former ones, but it was proving more and more difficult as the days went on. Dean would go the distance, making sure Qamal was cared for, and dinner was cooked before I got home so I could just spend a little time with them before hitting the books. Occasionally, he'd do something sweet like make a midnight picnic on our bedroom floor after getting the baby to sleep. We didn't have much, but what we have, he made look decadent. I'd put on lingerie, usually a clearance piece from Fredricks of Hollywood or Victoria's Secret, and he'd play one of my favorite records by D'Angelo, Maxwell, or Erykah Badu, and we'd talk until we could hardly keep our eyes open. Those nights were amazing; far and few in between.

His lack of understanding, my lack of communication, our disregard for the importance of trusting each other enough to share and be heard without judgment left a gaping hole in both of our hearts. It didn't help that I misinterpreted the signs of depression that he was showing as him just being an alpha male who was frustrated from the constant rejection when applying for consistent employment. Yet and still, our roller coaster lover affair wasn't even off the ground yet. In the next four years, we'd navigate all that goes with having multiple miscarriages and abortions, making our union legal by getting married on the hottest day of the year in July, ending friendships, and resisting forgiveness. All of this would occur between the birth of our son, Qamal, and our daughter Messiah who are 3 ½ years apart. Our life was a push and pull of two warriors on the same team weary from fighting the world and each other when the true war was within ourselves.

Warning, don't have celebration sex while you're ovulating, even if you are on birth control, and you use condoms. I found out I was pregnant with Messiah a few weeks after finishing my last final, a term early at Drexel. Evidently, those destiny kids will be created regardless of your best efforts. I was so happy to be finished early, had just been notified of my job offer, graduation was still three months away, and we'd just moved from our Germantown apartment to a cute little rental house that we didn't know was controlled by slum lords yet. Life was good until the pain hit. I kept getting fierce pains on my right side that wouldn't go away. By this point, I knew to take a pregnancy test, and of course, no surprise, I'm pregnant. Mr. Super-sperm has done it again, and I'm in tears, literally. We are finally at a point where our son isn't waking up every 20 minutes, there's a glimmer of light at the end of the struggle tunnel, and here I am, pregnant...again.

Normally, Dean and I are in sync with our frustration and anxiety about more kids. But this time, this dude was happy about it. Normally the pessimistic penny in the punch, he shocks me with his optimism. He said, "look, we can do this; our circumstances are so much better than they were before." Technically he was right, right? He was working at KYW, I' was working and already had an accepted offer to start in a few weeks at an adoption and foster care agency in the city, plus, we were renting a 3-bedroom house. So, what was I worried about? Ummm, try everything! For one, I wanted the freedom of starting my Psy.D program at Widener that fall without having two children on my hip. I was insistent on opening a private practice within ten years and knew accomplishing it with two kids would be twice as hard as before. For two, I was tired. School, plus, multiple jobs, plus internships, plus toddler, plus relationship is equivalent to a tired momma.

This Messiah of ours would stake her claim early and fervently regardless of my fatigued feelings. My doctor's visit, which confirmed the pain I endured was related to an unexpected pregnancy, would flip us on our head once again. Because my last menses, which was always irregular, was nearly four months prior, the vaginal exams dictation of fetal gestational age didn't line, so I had to get an ultrasound. That led to more "interesting observations" by the radiologist that led to us having to take a multi-day HCG blood test at the hospital. Dean and I spent a weekend in suspense. Were we pregnant? Was I miscarrying again? Do I simply have a big fibroid? Nope. After three long days, the doctor called us in to tell that my human chorionic gonadotropin (HCG) levels had more than tripled each day, indicating we were carrying twins. I was extremely early, and they could barely see the babies on the ultrasound the first time, so I'd need to come back in a few more weeks for a retake.

What in the world... Twins... Multiples again?!?! Both of our heads spinning, this time he's a bit less gleeful and more concerned. I have no problems getting pregnant, but my body doesn't always agree with me carrying to term, especially with multiples. Our anxieties were raised ten times, and I held onto a shame I couldn't share with him. I didn't think he could understand that as a woman, it was hard for me to deal with my body constantly betraying me, regardless of what my circumstances could allow for at the time. I want the option to choose to have or not to have, and that choice being taken from me, even by my own body, was hurtful. No one in my family had shared how common miscarriages were in our family and when doctors provided statistics, it always came with a sterile acknowledgment of normalcy followed by, "you can try again in a few months." Which would piss me off! Who the hell is trying to have kids at 18-23 years old, was always my thought? The facts would always get lunged over by disgust at their statements. And yet, here we are. Hoping that we wouldn't suffer another miscarriage but wondering what we'd do with two more children.

We sucked it up, told our family, and tried to prepare for a family of five. Our lives quickly turned the week of my undergraduate graduation. Dean lost his job at KYW, and a few weeks later, I was hit by a hit and run driver as I headed to a friends' house in West Philly for some girl time. Although it was never said definitively as the cause, Messiah's twin sister would die in utero. She kept trying to escape my womb after that day — a tenacious little girl, even before birth. After stopping my labor three times over the next few weeks, I was put on complete bed rest. In addition to this not being good for an ambitious mind who hasn't done her self-awareness work yet, our one household income couldn't handle the impact of this new mandatory prescription. Within a few months, Dean and I would move into his grandmothers' home and try to rebuild.

Our intimacy and the depth of our relationship were unthreading. We were used to being on our own, having our own space, and privacy. His grandmother had eleven adult children and countless grandchildren who loved her dearly and visited frequently. That alone was difficult for us to get used to. More importantly, it made it too easy to avoid dealing with us. We often defaulted into the unspoken understanding that certain conversations wouldn't be had if other people were in earshot, which was almost always. Already inherently different in our parenting styles, Dean more the nurture, and I, more the protective teacher, we both tightened the bubble around our kids. Leaning into more teachable moments than adventurous experiences, each with their creative personality would be nourished from the love we fed through a spoon of fear.

For thirteen months, we suffered in near silence, barely speaking to each other in-love, mostly just handling finances and having co-parenting conversations. Physical intimacy was extremely sporadic and occurred more out of our unapologetic needs than craving a deeper connection. The non-verbal wounds we were giving each other were beginning to leave marks. I had a few single and single-acting girlfriends that I'd confided in, not because they were the best to share with, but they were the ones who would take my side — not the smartest hour of my life, but definitely one of the more desperate ones. Over the next year, there would be severe post-partum depression, a second abortion, another miscarriage, another household move, and starting a master's degree program that would lead us to discover that we both wanted to live differently. Simply existing in the same space, was no longer enough.

# Section III Permission to Love

There are endless possibilities when we are willing to leap and fall and leap over and over again. If we're willing, to be honest, we'll admit that the wrestling that occurs between our heart, mind, spirit, and soul is sadistically pleasurable. When we embrace the process along our journeys', we uncover intimacy and run towards the gift, which is the permission to love, again and again.

# The Journey to Break Open

## 7

U p until this point, our lives were intertwined and misaligned. I was breaking down, mentally, and emotionally. Pulling further from the self that hadn't yet been discovered and what stood was unrecognizable to both of us. He had lost himself in parenthood, husbandry, and was falling deeper into depression, and I lost myself somewhere along the way in a flood of denial. We were physically in a new location but stuck in old patterns. I didn't have a clue at the time, but the imprint of my early childhood scripts of not feeling worthy of love was deepened with every trauma and the repeated acceptance of that story as truth. I resolved the ache attached to this false truth with justified proclamations when I'd tell myself, "that's just the way I way I am."

Just after we moved from Deans' grandmothers' home, we moved to a tiny house on Patton Street in the Grays Ferry section of South Philadelphia. We called that house, an apartment with stairs. It was small, but it had character. Open brick walls, hardwood floors, and horrible white popcorn ceiling, but it was home. Our fourth residence since leaving the small redbrick house in Mt. Airy, devoid of the old ghost but full of new demons. These demons were completely ours. On my 25th birthday, I woke up fighting one of those demons. I decided to take a shower, put on my overstuffed lavender robe, and clear my head. When I walked a few feet down the hall to our bedroom, I felt a rush of calm come over me, and I knew exactly what I needed to do. I leaned over the hallway banister and called down to Dean, asking him to come upstairs for a moment. As I waited, I went and sat on a small kente cloth covered milk crate we were using as mixed-used end table/footstool. When he came up, I looked at him and calmly said, "I need you to leave."

There was no big fight, no yelling or screaming, no pushing or pulling. There was Dean and me standing in the middle of a non-verbal agreement that it was time for us to live. At first, he didn't say anything. He went downstairs and grabbed a few black trash bags because, of course, we didn't own luggage or duffels larger than a single bookbag. He came back upstairs, opened the wooden sliding doors that led to our mini closet, and began dumping in his clothing. I sat quietly, completely still inward and outwardly. After he made a few trips downstairs, shuffling between full bags and bringing up empty ones, he walked over to me, leaned down, and said, "nothing I ever do for you is enough; you need to think about that." He was right, so there was no argument for me to have with him. It was exactly how I felt. Not that he wasn't enough, I felt he didn't do enough. He was pouring in all he could pour, but I was empty and exhausted from gushing out everything I had back into our life, and I felt alone in the process.

Dean and I are not people who renege or go back on our word. If we say we are going to do something or that we aren't going to do something, we follow it through. That's one of the few things we've always had in common. We both believe your word is not just everything; it's the only thing. So, when I asked him to leave, it was understood that our relationship was over for good. We were young and really didn't have money that extended beyond paying our bills, so the divorce process was really just a matter of us both putting money aside and getting the paperwork done. Neither of us needed to say it; we just knew that's what would be next. In the interim, we have these two incredible children, five and a half and a year and half old, who needed us to be all in with them, regardless of how broken we felt inside.

Fortunately, as people of our word, we had an agreement that went back to when I was four months pregnant with Qamal. Dean and I sat in my dorm at Drexel, in that private room on the sixth floor, and we agreed, in a near expected fashion, that should the moment come when we decided to break up, we'd co-parent without breaking our kid down. I can't tell you why we had the discussion earlier on in our relationship. There was no incident or issue between us to make us want to talk about it, other than the reality that we knew society expected us to fail. We were high school lovers who were sticking to each other like glue, young parents, and Black Americans. According to statistics, our love was unlikely to survive our twenty-first birthday, let alone the numerous trials and tribulations we'd triumphed through thus far.

The pack that we'd made in 1996 didn't need to be restated, it was understood. We were on what I affectionately refer to as a sabbatical for three months. Every weekday during that period, Dean would borrow his sister's car, come pick up the kids by 5 a.m., help get them dressed, and take them back to his mother's house so I could get ready for work. We had one car, and since I needed it for my case management job, clinical internship, and school, the car was with me. We didn't talk about those things; we just knew not to be spiteful to each other and do what was best for the family. Don't get me wrong, we were angry, and when we spoke on the phone, and the kids weren't in earshot, we would give each other some of the worse parts of ourselves. Cussing and fussing, bringing up hurtful comments or moments from the past, anything to highlight how one of us took the other for grant-ed. Still, every weekday, the ritual in play was to keep the kids with a healthy routine. Always attracted to each oth-er, even in our anger, there would be mornings Dean would arrive a little early to catch me coming out of the shower. We'd have we're not making up sex, and it would make our heads spin. Even so, we knew we needed to maintain space so we could discover ourselves for our-selves and not for each other.

During that sabbatical, I learned a lot about myself. I forgot how much I actually enjoyed Pilates, dancing, and being silly with the kids. I had become so serious and re-served. Dean not being in the house, forced me to see not only how much he contributed that I had taken for grant-ed, but it also forced me to see how much I could do with ease. There are things we stop doing, tell ourselves we don't do them, and they lose confidence at the thought of having to do them because it's been so long since we have done them. This was me with laundry. Dean had been do-ing the laundry since Qamal was six months old. I really thought I couldn't do it until I had to. This was also me staying up all night with a sick child. Dean and I was al-ways a well-oiled machine with the kids. We'd take turns without batting an eye, and if one of us looked like we were about to step over the edge from exhaustion, the other would double tap back in and give a little bit more to cover the other. I wasn't sure I could do it without him until I did. Guess what; I was absolutely fine.

## Leaping, Falling, and Leaping Again

Being a single parent for that short time frame was tough. What I realized about myself during that time was that I had become egocentric to hide my truth. I was scared to sit down with Dean and tell him that I was feeling overwhelmed, irritable, restless, depressed, hopeless, and that I couldn't shut my thoughts off. I was fully immersed in postpartum depression (PPD) and I didn't want to admit it. I didn't want him to tell me to take a semester off from school, to slow down, or quit one of my three jobs. We both knew the reason I was doing what I did was that I was trying to offset what wasn't coming in. Ever since his accident, he'd had a difficult time getting full-time employment beyond contract or staffing positions. They would look at his hand and assume he had a disability or would be a liability, so they'd sidestep his resume and default him to mailroom clerk positions or anything else that would have him out of sight.

The wages were low, and the gaps between employment were wide, so I maintained as many professional side hustles as necessary to make ends meet. In the behavioral science world, you won't come close to making money that could reasonably pay rent in a halfway decent neighborhood unless you have a graduate degree, kiss the right ring, or have over ten years' experience in the field; preferably all three. A two-year full-time master's degree program was essential for our income goals. Especially now that I'd side-stepped the doctorate degree to have Messiah and build additional cashflow before going back to school. Talking to Dean about my PPD symptoms would make him feel like things he couldn't control were his fault, and they weren't. So instead, in a twisted way, I would just focus on the things that were his fault and in his control. In my backward way, I defaulted to my child-hood scripts of saving and protecting instead of helping myself first. If I would've just talked to him, we would've likely handled that period of our lives differently. But this was my growth through to get to the other side of the lesson.

It may have been a bit early in the process, but I leaped. I did something I've never done before and went against my word. Fully intended on being completely done with Dean romantically, being clear we were headed for divorce just three "official years" into our marriage, I leaped and asked him to come back home so we could try to work things through. He was extremely hesitant, and for weeks, he said he'd need to think about it because he was also discovering and rediscovering himself. As time moved closer to our son's 6th birthday, he agreed to come home if we would both work at communicating more openly.

Of course, when he returned home, it was awkward. The kids were too young for us to have to over-explain the sabbatical, so they fell right in tow with their pre-breakup routine. We, however, were on eggshells with each other. Both of us were now overly thankful, overly gracious for everything, and overly cautious. It was as if we were waiting for the other glass shoe to break. The in-authenticity of this supposedly better us didn't last long. We finally broke open the basement door of our feelings and shared what we were afraid of. We talked. Really talked for the first time in a long time about boundaries. What we needed from and for each other so our 25-year-old selves could breathe, lean into the good and find more. We had been holding each other to the younger version of ourselves and not welcoming each other's growth. That stagnation was smothering our spirits and our dreams. Now that we were honest, I could stop fighting him so hard and relax into the safety that had al-ways been a presence, but I had been scripted not to see. I permitted myself to love, allowing myself an opportunity to embrace a mustard seed portion of what I deserved the moment I allowed love in.

A few months after I graduated with my Master's de-gree from Bryn Mawr Graduate School of Social Work and Social Research and sat for my LCSW exam, my baby brother, now thirteen, called in crisis. He'd come home to find my mother in an intimate-partner violence dispute with a young man only a few years older than him. He got in the middle of it, the glass table broke into pieces, and with it, his tolerance to continue to live with my mother and her substance abuse addiction. He asked to come stay with Dean and I. Without hesitation, we said yes and went to retrieve him. Putting up a little more of a fight than she did with me as a child, my mother tried to convince me that my brother was fine and just didn't want to deal with her barely existent rules any longer. Worried that her welfare benefits would be cut short and her section-8 housing affected due to his removal, she was less than friendly about me bringing him home. Consistently inconsistent, her fight dissipated, which was confirmed when she didn't show up for court at the temporary custody hearing. By defaulted judgment, my brother was now fully, legally in my care. Dean and I now were the parents of three.

Raising my brother was no easy task. He came with a host of patterns and habits that, although were familiar, were intolerable in the bubble we'd created for our children. We had structure, bedtimes, chores, expectations, and as he got older, curfews. After six years of trying to get us to bend to his will, he left me a "Dear John" letter, telling me how much he loved all of us, but needed the freedom that my mother could give him. I chuckled a bit when I read the letter; it was so filled with so much of the sentiment that I had towards my grandmother when she told me she couldn't deal with me anymore at 12 years old. Now here he was at 19, voicing his needs for the same freedom. Clearly, some things from my grandmother were showing up in my parenting after all.

I knew I needed to let my baby brother follow his own journey of leaping and falling, and felt like he was at least old enough, with enough tools to do so. The focus was fully on our nuclear family now. I was torn, feeling completely disconnected from my original goal to open a small private practice. Dean and I would ebb and flow in our marriage, typical to how marriages do, and we were committed to trying to trust each other to love one another with all we could muster. Neither of us believed in unconditional love, we each had conditions. I needed for the kids and me to always be safe, and he needed to be seen and heard without assumptions or judgments. We both had our baggage to unpack, and neither of us had the capacity to hold onto anything else that belonged to the other. Because we were brutally honest about that, our love would live another day.

The kids would grow older, test us more, and more often. Our oldest was the quiet, introverted creative, who saw the world in a uniquely genius way. So, like his father that way, but with a more restless spirit. He would do things like write his name backward, then stand in front of the mirror, holding his name so he could read it the right way through the mirror. He was 3-years old the first time he did that, and he's been doing things back to see them right in his own eyes ever since. Our youngest was a bit of a ham when she was younger, loved being in front of the camera, a multi-talented performer, and all too-literal rule follower. Qamal, our oldest, would have to deal with finding ways to have quiet fun because we spent a lot of time at the doctors with his sister. She had always had something peculiar going on with her immune system and inner workings that would lead to tests, specialists, diagnosis, and more tests. Between their completely different personalities, all our appointments, their activities, work, and conversations about the next steps in my mind, our plates were overflowing with busyness. I truly had no time to be stuck or confused, but that's where I was.

By this point, I had well over a decade of experience in my field, had niched down in trauma-informed care, human behavior, relationship management, with quite a few other certifications under my belt, and I'd convinced myself that my previous passion to be Dr. Webster Thigpen was still important. To avoid breaking expectations that I'd set for myself, I started an accredited doctoral program online through Widener University's Public Health program. For personal reasons, I was extremely interested in the relationship between self-care, corporate stress, and their support systems, better known as work/life balance programs. Although I was equally interested in studying postpartum depression and work/life balance, I decided to move with the former for my dissertation. Doing well academically, I tried to tell myself that this was the path I needed to be on to fill the void I felt inside. That abyss widened every time I refuse to break free from expectations that no longer served me, including those of my previous passions, but I didn't know how to let go. Always loyal to a fault.

A few years prior, four of my beyond blood sisters, were separately but harmoniously pouring into me, sharing the peace they'd receive from believing in God. Each, playing a different position in my life, with a unique and reciprocal relationship, could see a fragmented spirit and urged me to at least visit a church. Stubborn, young, and overly educated, I goaded them each to leave me be, and keep their God to themselves. With so much knowledge in my head about religion, layered on top of the hypocrisies demonstrated by people who claim to love God's children, it was irrefutably difficult for me to consider praising a power that would allow such evil in the world. After all, my mother's youngest sister, the fierce advocate of the family, had introduced me to Jesus when I was twelve years old, and I'd been tussling with her prayers over me ever since I left the church at fifteen.

Nonetheless, wanting to support my godson, who was scheduled to mime a worship song with the youth choir, I finally visited my best friend's church service. I was surprised at how kind and authentic everyone seemed. When asked, I accidentally told the Pastor that I would be back. As soon as I said it, I regretted letting the words falling from my lips.

Keeping my word has always meant everything to me, and as you know, letting go, my pattern of loyalty was a constant struggle. I showed up the following Sunday, and then every Sunday that I wasn't working in the Emergency room after that. Not one to half-do anything, I didn't want to play church or pretend that I was committed to something I couldn't embrace fully. As a curious bunny rabbit, always hopping from question to question, in search of the juiciest carrot, I asked God to show me something unshakeable, proof of his existence and love for me that I could never deny. Within a few months, he did just that. I experienced the Holy Spirit at a level that you'd need to be a witness in the room to understand. To this day, the thought of that moment warms my soul. At that very minute, my spirit was re-centered and anchored to the unconditional love of God.

Dean was raised Episcopalian and wasn't much into the pomp and circumstance that can come with today's non-denominational churches. Although he visited a few with the kids and me, we agreed his path would be his own and my tenacious pattern to try and convince him that my way was the best wouldn't work in this realm of his life. It would take me more than a few years to swallow a pill of understanding in this area, but with time, I did, and his relationship with God grew stronger without my input, as did my love for him. Nonetheless, in this hour of my life, I was stuck!

A year into my doctorate program, I had been asking God to show me what I was placed on this earth to do. My specific prayer was, "God, show me **what** I am supposed to do here." In reflection, I should have asked him to show me how to do it. But you live, and you learn.

## The Vision

On July 11th, 2009, I stood amid my fellow congregation members at Freedom Christian Bible Fellowship Church in West Philadelphia and saw my life change in front of my eyes. I had officially joined Freedom in January of the same year, after being led there by the Holy Spirit, guiding me like a loose flower petal floating on the ocean waters, with complete ease and flow. Over that time, I was wrestling with myself, trying to figure out the direction I should go into next because on paper, success wasn't what defined me. By all accounts, I looked pretty good on paper and should've been content, considering the depths of hand over fist feeding frenzy Dean and I had just gone through. I had my Masters degree, I was licensed, highly sought after in and outside my main job at the Children's

Hospital of Philadelphia, we were new homeowners, didn't have to pinch pennies to buy food and groceries, and both of our babies were healthy! Anyone who knew our story would've smacked me at the thought of saying there is more. Yet, I knew it was so much more out there for me to do, be, achieve, and receive.

With all the good that was around me, I didn't feel like I was walking in my Godly purpose. I knew things weren't as they should be because I wasn't in alignment. My work/life balance was completely off-tilt. I loved the work I did but wasn't in love with the limits of my position. In my core positions at CHOP, I worked in the Emergency Room, Special Delivery Unit, Neonatal Care Unit, Inpatient Endocrinology, and on the Sexual Assault Response Team (SART). My fundamental role as a medical clinical social worker was to manage the crisis, listen for the needs, provide support, and direct towards resources. All the things I loved doing (and) there were restrictions to the support I could provide, which hindered my ability to serve people on the deepest and greatest level that I knew I could. There were times when couples would be at capacity with the amount of stress they'd endure because of the financial hardships, inconveniences, and emotional tax they succumbed to from their caregiving experiences.

Many of the issues that would explode into crisis would stem from a misunderstanding that was bred from guilt, frustration, and anxiety. They'd lash out on each other, mostly verbally, and often, families would crumble from the weight of it all. As a psychotherapist, I would help them navigate some of the communication challenges and provide resources to support them with help with lodging, medical bills, transportation, and whatever else I could. But many of the things I couldn't officially help them with was strategizing solutions, especially if they were connected to business or leadership issues. That wasn't covered under the hospital's professional liability insurance, and needless to say, I wasn't a business or leadership strategist, so I had to be extremely mindful of inferences, let alone things that could be construed as direct advice while representing the hospital. For me, they were basic creative productivity and efficiency in workflow problem-solving solutions, but for the hospital, it could have led to lawsuits or other legalistic nightmares. What I heard the most from families was how much they missed time for each other, but one or both parents were so busy building their legacies or just trying to pay bills, that there was no room left for balancing the things that mattered most to them.

I wasn't interested in leaving my doctorate program to get an MBA, and I knew the core of who I am was connected to my active listening skills as a clinician, my talents for creative designing, and my gift of problem solving. From a surface standpoint, I was already in the right field and doing the right thing. I design solutions to problems, so what, in fact, was my problem with doing it the way it was already being done? That was the billion-dollar question. What I could tell you is that I felt like my legs were stuck in the mud and the air around me was tart, sticky, and repulsive. I began to feel trapped, and like anyone or anything that feels trapped, I started to rebel against everything and everyone.

Dean and I were pretty good before I started feeling strapped, so he, of course, being the closest to me, got the worse of my rebellion. He wasn't all sugarplums and apple pie easy to deal with all the time, but I must admit, at that time in my life, I was more than a little handful. At work, I found myself disengaged in anything that wasn't patient facing, and no longer wanted to volunteer with the groups I was previously passionate about helping, like the teens with sickle cell disease that I had grown such a heart for or some of the external committees and boards I led. I started peeling things off my plate and pushing people away. I fell into a deeply isolated bubble and the only voice I could hear was my own. That was until the Holy Spirit called me out and wrapped with a warmth that I can't quite describe to you. It was bright, vibrating, warm and firm. It was as if God instructed the universe to gift me with a perfectly shaped, soft- heated-velvet weighted blanket on a cold day while whispering that I was his favorite. It's the best visual I can give you at that moment and I pray you felt it.

The day my life changed, when I felt the first paradigm shift occur under my feet, a prophetic benediction and prayer were being led by Bishop Coleman at the head of the church. I could hear him speaking and see my fellow brothers and sisters in Christ walking to the front to receive a special prayer over their lives. The directive by the Bishop was to come to the front of the church if you needed a prayer of clarity around your purpose. Not quite in those exact words, but that was the gist of his directive. As I went to stand up and walk towards the aisle to go to the front, my feet were clamped to the floor. Just as I went to look down to see what the heck was holding my feet still, I had a 3D like spiritual download. While others were being called up to receive prayer for clarity, the answer to my question, that I had repeated to God nearly every day for close to a year, was being delivered to my soul. Remember earlier, I shared with you that I asked God to show me *"what"* I am supposed to do here as my purpose on this earth. That's exactly the answer I received. Like watching a movie play on a large movie screen, I could see the self-care focused institute I would one day create and the floors and rooms within it. There was a small part of me that understood some of the things I saw, which were symbolic and not literal, but I didn't put much emphasis on the symbolism at the time.

I went home that afternoon, walking on air. My energy was the highest it had been in forever, and I couldn't wait to share with Dean. I could barely hold it in when I walked in the door that afternoon, but I knew I needed to commit what I saw to paper. I grabbed my black & white fabric color journal and sketched its eye in the form of a mind map before I bothered to take off my shoes. Although it wasn't intentional, the flow of the words that comprised the mind map was in the shape of a tree. I put my pen down, and immediately, the tears of joy streamed down my face. Trees were one of my private signs for hope, growth, and escape. When I was a little girl, I use to stare out the back window of the small redbrick house in Mt. Airy, stare at and sketch the trees that towered over the houses of the neighboring block. As I grew older and away from sketching in pencil, I'd doodle with painting those trees from memory, then eventually just memorializing them in my mind. For me, seeing the layout, the vision I received, etched in the shape my hope was unarguable confirmation.

## Reflect & Celebrate
*Lessons Learned*

Therapy, spiritually grounded support circles, creative outlets, forgiving yourself, and the wisdom that you need to be pulled forth by something bigger than yourself are all a part of life's healing cocktail.

Don't be shy. Drink up.

# Pouring from an Empty Cup

**8**

H ere lies the problem with ambitious folks. When we have an inch, we run the mile so fast we miss exit that would've given us our next juicy clue for where we need to go next. I was amped up from a spiritual clarity high that I sped right by the next huge exit marker that told me exactly what I needed to do next, trust. As someone who fed off being in control, trusting what I couldn't see, touch, or taste, didn't come easy. So, I did what I knew to do; I took matters into my own hands and put my faith in what I could see. Next step, complete a SWOT analysis of my skills to examine all my strengths and weaknesses. I knew the personal development side of the business would be easy to develop because of my profession. But, and the big but was that I didn't know how to start or grow a business.

The volume inside my head turned up. I leaned into all the negative thoughts about what I didn't have, what I couldn't do, and all that I didn't know. That pessimism pulled me further from the tears of joy I cried just a few weeks earlier when my emotional battery was charged with hope. I felt all the feels that go with hearing your inner gremlins tell you that you aren't enough. Searching for the light, I dug a hole in the wall of my fear and jumped into an abyss, only it was another level of lack of trust waiting on the other side. That evening I convinced myself that I needed to leave the hospital and go work for a company that would challenge me to deepen my leadership capabilities and build business acumen.

My trust in God and the purpose that was pulling me forth was being calcified over with the misguided belief that I wasn't worthy of the vision that I both asked for and received. I denied that I was called to claim my destiny; instead, I convinced myself that I wasn't ready and needed to qualify myself. The truth was, I wasn't scared of failing; I was afraid of succeeding. Inherently, I understood that with greater rewards come greater responsibility. My plates were full and stacked with more plates on top of each other. Between Dean, the kids, my full-time job, full-time enrollment in the doctoral program, residencies, weekend shifts as an EAP counselor for the military, evening shifts training therapist who worked with families whose children had behavioral or developmental challenges, and volunteering at church, my cup was running dry. There was nothing left to give, so how could I have room for more of anything, let alone, more of what I wanted or deserved? Running on empty nearly every day for the last 13 years, trying to just survive, I had nothing left to give and when I'd squeeze something out, it was scraped from my insides. Pouring from an empty cup, left me open to receive everything except my next level of greatness.

## Buzzing Bees Go Boom

Never one to be timid about jumping, I leaped out of CHOP and into a new position at a new company a little more than a year after I received the vision of what my future could hold. On paper, the opportunity looked like what I *thought* I needed and came with the added benefit of being in center city, only about a mile and a half from the kids' school. At this new opportunity, I would come face to face with my first Queen Bee. Oh, she was hot with me, from the first day I started working. I didn't know it at the time, but because she was out sick on the day I interviewed with all 27 plus staff members, she was furious that I was hired without her input. On my first day, she was waiting for me, hovering with a nice smile to conceal her intentions. I swear someone rolled her character right out of the book of Baal and rewarded her with an Oscar for most authentic performance as the best demon to play human ever.

Ella, as I'll call her, was my supervisor. She was smart, had a tight rapport with the final decision-makers in the organization and stakeholders across the city of Philadelphia. Within the first few weeks, I realized she was feared more than respected by the other employees. Conveniently for her, at that time in my life, I was still at the people-pleasing point of my life. Always smiling, creating ways to give even though I was empty on the inside, I attracted quite a few of the team members towards me and developed a good rapport. Ella didn't seem to appreciate my cheery disposition, nor the friendliness people reciprocated. Like all women with Queen Bee syndrome, she couldn't see an ally, co-leader, or good asset; she simply saw me as a competitor coming for her resources. It didn't help that I wasn't challenged by the work as I had hoped to be. A trial by fire style onboarding, I was thrown into the work with a few shadows and introductions, and then told to get started! A natural leader, I jumped in, learned quickly, and attracted attention as one to watch. Queen Ella noticed the buzz around me and lunged in with an attack that would backfire for both of us.

The morning of the attack began no different than any other. Determined to drop my 2nd baby, doctoral journey weight gain, I woke up at 4:15 a.m., drove to my 5 a.m. spin class in Springfield, got home, showered, nudged the kids along to school and then went to work. I was in an energetic mood, likely because I had been working on bringing in a few new expert trainers for the professional development training series I organized. One of my roles as the head of training and development, so when I curated new talent to bring in fresh content for the lawyers and social workers internal to our group, there was always a touch of excitement that would add a little sparkle to my day. I just wrapped up the confirmation of one of those new speakers, so I sent an email to the company email list notifying them of the topic and logistics and asked that they sign up if they were interested in the sign-up sheet posted outside my door. Only I hadn't put the sign-up sheet out yet. After printing it up, I walked outside my office door with two small pieces of clear scotch tape in hand and taped it to my smooth brown wooden door. As I went to add the bottom piece of tape to secure the sheet, Ella screamed at me to stop and came rushing towards me like a bulldog. As she closed in, yelling, she vomited out the words, "We don't do that here, you can't put anything on the door." A little context here, EVERY office door on our floor was filled with some sort of art or personal touch that gave an appearance of welcomed energy and warmth. There were pictures of people's children, pleasant motivational sayings, and the like, literally on every door, except mine.

Back to the Boom. As Ella rushed towards me and got so close, I could smell what she ate for breakfast; I had an outer body experience. I was triggered, and fortunately for Ella, I was aware of the trigger. Her scream and rush toward me pulled me back to childhood violence. I saw myself climb up the front of her face, wrap myself around her back and tighten my hands around her throat. As the .02 second out of body image played across my mind, I caught it, and myself from escalating into a full-on explosion. I stepped back, looked at Ella, as I pressed my hands into the sheet that I tore from the door to keep my fist from balling up, I looked into her soul, and with the calmest voice said, "you should be careful not to get into someone's personal space, you never know what you might trigger." Ella took a big step back and said, she was sorry, then went into some hypocritical mention of why I couldn't put a sign-up sheet on the door because it was against policy, one I'd never seen nor been informed about. I remember shaking my ahead okay and asked her to come into my office so we could talk. My hands still pressed and mind still battling to suppress the boom that was rising from the bottom of my toes.

When we walked in, she closed the door behind us. I thought to myself; she really doesn't know what she's doing and has completely confused me. A small office, ironically, no bigger than a jail cell, I walked over to the front of my desk and sat in one of the two chairs that would encourage her to sit next to me instead of me sitting across from her. Queen Ella didn't sit. She stood, hands on hips, face flushed red, and was careful not to come within arms reach of me. The expression on my face was transparent, and we were going to have a grown-ass woman conversation. Political correctness be damned. Her face was also transparent, and it was clear that she realized she made a mistake when she brazenly closed the door behind us.

## Nice & Dumbfounded

Ella expressed that she thought I was working at the organization with a secret goal to take her job. She mentioned that it didn't make sense that I would have any other plan, especially considering I was working on my doctorate and already had a ton of certifications. Ella could see that I was ambitious, and she believed that I'd use that ambition to take what belonged to her. Only that I didn't want it. I had my plans and it didn't involve her or her titles. She looked dumbfounded when I told her emphatically that my dreams were larger than the three-floor building we stood in and the only thing I wanted from her was to respect my personal space or risk a response that neither of us would benefit from. With both confusion and compulsion, Queen Ella turned around and immediately left my office.

Our conversation was extremely revealing. Queen Ella came at me for two reasons, I appeared to be easy prey and she thought there wasn't enough greatness to go around for the both of us. I wore the disease to please mask over my savior complex and it gave off signals of susceptibility. I wore it mostly at work and thought it was a better accessory than my tattered save a chick Cape or misplaced rage. Sometimes the symptom of this disease to please, is that you are much nicer than you are kind. When you come across as nice, people often mistake this as weak, easy to get over on, and assume you don't have the skill or gull to choke them out...

My later grow thru process helped me understand that being nice was typically what broken people painted on top of whatever mask they wore to camouflage their pain. It helped them blend in and lessened the chances of anyone discovering their insecurities or self-identified in-adequacies. Niceness was superficial and inauthentic. Kind people are vulnerable, strong, gentle, and honest. But you can only become a kind person if you learn to be kind to yourself first. It would be a lot of work and a long time before I'd get from nice to courageous kindness. And I wasn't there yet.

Fortunately for Queen Ella, and my future self, a few years prior to our near explosion, I had begun therapy and was learning to forgive myself, and be kinder to my inner child. Had it not been for the work I had begun so many years earlier and the God that covered me from even the enemy within myself, I would probably be writing this book from the inside of a jail cell. Because I recognized that Ella rushing over to me was a trigger that would normally cue a physical response to fight, I could give my inner child a reality check, talk to her with a little kindness and point out that there was no need for the little warrior to react in a state of fear. There was no threat here that I couldn't handle with words first. However, with all the work I was doing on myself, I was still very much still on the side of the continuum where I was more "nice Kia," the people-pleasing child who really wanted to save everyone over herself. Queen Ella was meeting me at the bridge where I stood between the child that needed healing and the woman, Naketa, who had been healed. The therapeutic and God graced bricks that built that bridge saved us both that day. Without the courage to be kind to myself, my life would've gone boom.

# Section IV:
# Permission to Laugh

Discovering the boundless limitations of where our un-
bound brilliance can take us is electrifying. Yet, it's difficult to conceive of building what we may not believe we
are worthy of enjoying. Every day, we move so fast and
smile so little. We move through the world with such ferocious seriousness and rarely slow down to create memories. Permission to laugh is what all of us could use a little daily dose of. It will minimize the ache of uncontrollable elements in our reality.

# The Breakthrough

## 9

Three months later, I was miserable. Although Queen Ella and I were respecting our unspoken understanding to stay clear of each other at work as much as you can in a 30-person company, there was a shift, and I was rocked by it. There was an action step directed from that experience that I needed to take, only I didn't know what it was. There was so much noise from the busyness of my life, and it drowned out the messages God was sharing with me through the Holy Spirit. Every sign from the universe that signaled me to slow down, pause, look, or listen, I ran right by, searching for answers I could touch.

The workload from my doctoral classes was beginning to intensify as I was getting closer to the start of dissertation prep, our new house was falling apart at the seams, one electrical, plumbing or roofing issues at a time, and the bills were piling up. I was so furious with myself for not asking God the right question. I felt so lost, and although I now had immense clarity on the what of my purpose, I needed guidance on "how" to get from where I was, to where I knew I was meant to be. I'd become more rigid and structured my schedule in a way I thought would help me balance my life better.

My calendar became my second bible, and the goal to fit everything in was my new pastor. Intentional not to take a phone call longer than ten minutes if I had the kids in the car, coordinating dinner with daily recipe nights posted on the fridge to hold myself accountable to cook at least four days/week, and scheduling sex for three days/week. It was all part of my master plan to make room for whatever was coming next. There were some things I did right, attempting to make room was smart. The way I went about it was quite neurotic. I 10x'd my weekend warrior parenting, took the kids to every birthday party, playdate, church event, and family gathering we were invited to, whether they wanted to attend or not. I was intent on creating memories come hell or high water. In my mind, they'd appreciate it later and see that I was showing them they mattered most. Messiah, my daughter's words to me just a few years earlier, never left my mind. I kept hearing her say, "you're awesome, you're just awesome for everyone else..."

Brilliant and unbalanced, most nights I spent tossing and turning, restless, mind ruminating over the millions of possible things I could do to jump into creating the self-care institute I'd envisioned almost two years ago. My brain would twirl with thoughts of everything from net-work marketing to gain capital to seed in the business, to convincing myself I should open a part-time private prac-tice, through trying to convince myself that I should pick up extra shifts to stuff in the hours that I wasn't using since I clearly couldn't sleep! I was on a spiral downhill and fast, and it felt like the fall would never end. One night, a little after 10 p.m., still slipping and sliding in my mind, body, soul, and life, my spirit got caught on some-thing. Desperate to stop the dizziness from constant fall-ing, I thought this was my eureka and saving grace!

The epiphany occurred to me while I was working on another 20+ page paper for school. Having a hard time staying centered and focused on the task at hand, my mind wandered, and in true pretend-productivity fashion, I began checking emails. In my inbox were not one, not two, but three different emails asking me if I knew anyone who was hiring. Known as a resource within my personal and professional network, nothing about this was unusu-al, except the number and the timing. Because I held so many jobs and researched a ton for clients, I'd come across opportunities all the time. Though usually, I'd get maybe one or two requests a week, on this night, there were three staring back at me. The idea struck that be-cause everyone already sees me as a resource, and we've always wanted to help people create more financial stabil-ity to give their families a chance to stay together and whole, why not open a staffing agency! Wooooooh! This makes total sense, right? To be sure, I went to confirm it with my soul's half, my husband.

Dean was always brutally honest with me, and quite the contrarian. If I said the sky was blue that morning, he and all his intelligence would point out that it was teal with a hint of green... I knew I could count on him shooting down anything that wasn't anchored in possibility, and I needed his raw truth that night. Our little 1516 square foot corner home had two main floors excluding the basement. Sitting on the floor of our bedroom, with my laptop propped on my lap, and Dean right downstairs in the living room beneath me, I did what any other 21st century wife would do. I sent him a text message. I text, "what about opening a staffing agency." Intrigued, he replied, "come here." Now, I knew this chat could either be comprised of me trying to convince him and myself why it was an excellent way to jump into entrepreneurship to create our financial freedom, or he'd simply shut it down with all the reasons it didn't make sense.

Neither of those things happened that night. Dean was in a job at a national law firm (no, he's not a lawyer), that exhausted him mentally and physically. He was doing work that he was really good at, and also not in love with. Far from his creative car, he was craving freedom as well. This night was a perfect storm of desperation for both of us. I didn't need to convince him to run for the door; he was already there. So that night, we talked for hours and had to tell ourselves to stop and go to bed. It was May 9, 2011, and we'd just conceived our next baby; only this one would be a baby business. We agreed that it would likely take at least a year to get everything together logistically and legally, and we were both excited to see the exit sign pointing "this way to freedom" blinking in our mind. We *thought* we'd fell onto the how...

There was a new vulnerability pushing through. At my core, I was frightened of what this new wedge of space was in my life. Completely uncomfortable and foreign to me, there was a dichotomy to it that didn't align with what I had understood about it up until this point. How could I feel so open and exposed, yet relieved by it all? To say it was a weird but exhilarating time in my life would be a complete underrepresentation. I tussled with it, trying to take control when the feeling pushed up from the inside, especially during unusual times. The first time I noticed the openness was when I jumped in Dean's suitcase on one of his work trips to Denver. I'd never been there and had an ache to break free from work for a few days and just be. Without the kids and responsibilities or expectations that came with day to day life. As an ambitious woman with absolutely zero balance, regardless of how many things I'd schedule and overschedule in my calendar, I didn't truly understand how to do that, just be, and

I knew I needed it. Of course, I did just the opposite when I got to Denver...

Dean worked 16-18-hour days while we were there. The law firm he worked for was expanding, and as one of the key projects' leaders, he was responsible for managing the flow to make sure they could move to a bigger space without disrupting client services. That left me quite a few hours to myself, so I took advantage. We'd already received our official LLC paperwork and EIN a few weeks earlier, so my ego was boosted a bit. I doubled down on writing a business plan, 68 pages long and called Harrisburg federal government offices to learn about corporate taxes and what our business would need to get off the ground successfully with headquarters in Philadelphia, Pennsylvania. By the end of that trip, where I was supposed to give myself permission to pause and just be, I felt accomplished. I returned home with a few more appointments on my calendar, time to go to the Small Business Association, appointments with Wharton University's Business School to get help finding flaws in the business plan, and a few others. Off to the races, with a limp in my gut, I went.

I didn't feel completely connected to the idea of starting a staffing agency, so we added a second division on paper. After the first division of staffing services had some legs under it, we'd expand the second division, professional development services that would develop leaders.

We didn't want to call it leadership development because we wanted to work with entrepreneurs who wanted to become better leaders in their business as well as traditionally defined leaders who worked inside hierarchical organizations. In a marketing effort to seed the second division in the minds of our prospective clients, instead of offering coffee mugs and pens as freebies, we'd give them free mini-workshops, about a half-hour long. I was amped! We had a great plan, and all of the business leaders and established folks I spoke to agreed it was flawless, especially given that we had time to lay it out. Remember, Dean and I agreed that it would be at least a year before we opened the doors.

## Flip the Fear & Break Barriers

Three days before my 34th birthday, I went to my meticulously scheduled back to back annual doctors' appointments. Spaced apart with m.u.d room in between (leaving time to manage any unavoidable delays), the morning was carved out for my gynecological visit the primary well check to follow in the early afternoon. What seemed to begin as a straight and narrow day, ended with a sharp left and a major pothole halt. I nearly ignored the gynecologist when she said I had several hard lumps in both breasts. This wasn't my regular doctor, and I needed to believe she was somehow unfamiliar with the fibrous tissues that African American women tend to have. When she handed me the prescription to schedule a mammogram, I dismissed her with a quibble response that I'd talk to my doctor later that afternoon first. Which is exactly what I didn't do. Working in healthcare for the majority of my career, I know how quick physicians are to follow breadcrumbs already provided, even if it leads them in the wrong direction.

Feeling a bit anxious on my way to the afternoon appointment, I decided to pull over and pray. It was a hot day in July, and our car's air conditioner wasn't that strong, yet I knew I needed to stop in give thanks. I praised God for all that's been done for our family and all that we'd continue to receive. Praying the heavens down over myself and asked God to send angels to cover our family if it would be the will of God for me to endure a diagnosis that my mind couldn't wrap my head around. I prayed for miracles to flood our family, and everyone connected to us in that hour. As an intercessor, someone who is steadfast in praying for others even when they can't, I needed to include everyone connected to us to ensure the blessings would ripple through and around me. So that's what I did, calling out everyone that mattered to me by name. I nearly missed my afternoon well check sitting in the car for over an hour, praying down the heavens and praising God for all that he had already provided. By the time I was done, I was drained, but it was the best feeling in the world. All my fears had been emptied. I knew that no matter what, I could handle whatever was next.

With a bit of context, this was the same year one of my maternal aunts, barely in her mid-40's had just had a double mastectomy a few months earlier. I'd also known my maternal grandmother had several biopsies at various times for breast cancer, and my mother reportedly had cancer a few years prior. I can only say reportedly because there were many things my mother mentioned about her health that weren't necessarily grounded with the truth. So, when my primary physician, completed her full well check and said she was concerned about lumps that she discovered, and I'd refused to tell her about, I knew I needed to share the earlier doctors' findings. My doctor was a tiny tough Haitian woman who didn't hold back or worry about being politically correct when she spoke. After she cleared her throat and told me that I needed to acquire genetic testing in addition to the mammogram, I smiled and said, "but I know I'm fine, I already prayed on it and have peace about it." The physician looked at me and said, I'm sure you are covered in the blood of Jesus, and he allowed us to have these tests for a reason. A kick in the pants from a beautiful bold spirit, I got dressed and immediately scheduled my mammogram before I left the doctor's office.

Just the thought that I could have cancer was the catapult that forced me to question what I'd done with my life thus far. I hadn't truly lived, I rarely laugh, and I was not doing all that I was created to do. The fear that I thought had been drained from me through praise and prayer had flipped. I used it to break the barrier façade that was my comfort zone and leaped into entrepreneurship, head-on. I went home and told Dean about the two doctors' appointments and how I refused to half-live my life any further. If I was going to have some short life span, it was going to be on my own terms. I was emphatic that I needed to hand in my week resignation on Monday. As I said before, Dean has always been the more logistical, how will this work in real-time half of my soul. But he is indeed my soul's half. He could see the passion and fire in my eyes. I was determined, so instead of pointing out the 1ooo's of reasons I should wait or rethink my decision to open the company doors immediately, he supported me through the transition ahead.

On Monday, the director and I were scheduled to attend a meeting at a suburban set facility that was interested in our company training their staff in one of the personal development programs I'd designed for emerging leaders in healthcare. It was a fantastic meeting, the director fell back and allowed me to take the lead with pitching the value and importance personal growth tenants would have on not only the staff but the clients they support. After our great meeting, we went to lunch, and I handed him my six weeks' notice. It would become one of the most empowering moments that helped my transition. Because of all the great work that I'd done in my short duration with the organization, I was an irrefutable asset. I didn't just know it inherently; the director told me and asked me to reconsider my resignation. Without getting into the personal reasons that catapulted me to that moment, I told him that I needed to lend my talents to our family business and reveled at the reality that I'd just created the first of many opportunities to say no. It was unfortunate that it took the fear of death, the possibility of leaving my children and my husband with more medical bills than memories, for me to get out of my head long enough to see what was right in front of me. The day I hit the bottom of my life was at the moment, I thought it could all end before I was ready. That was the day my breakthrough began.

# Addicted to Surviving

## 10

Breakups are hard. Nevertheless, if you're in an unhealthy, let alone toxic relationship, for your sanity and future, breaking up is essential. If all of us are honest with ourselves, we'll admit that it's not an unknowing that keeps us tethered in these less than desirable relationships. Most of the time, we see but choose to ignore all the red flags, especially the ones that come with their fire alarms to sound off the danger ahead. After a while, we're so used to the high pitch sound that it becomes soothing white noise in the backgrounds of our lives. There's comfort in the adrenaline rush brought on by familiar drama. Although there are periods, we reach maximum capacity for the nonsense and its related rolled out consequences, trying to rationalize with an unhealthy person who's an expert at gaslighting and manipulating you into a fetal position, isn't always worth the energy. Sometimes, it's just easier to avoid the conflict by justifying the negative behaviors with a sort of declassification system. If we minimize behavior "*x*" as not being *too horrible* compared to behavior "z," followed by absent-minded remembrance of the frequency of which z-behavior occurred compared to x-behavior, well look at that, the relationship isn't so bad after all right?

What's most intriguing is that many of us eventually get to the point where we have had enough, eventually ending the one relationship, only to fall into another version of that bad relationship later down the line. Each time, we recognize the signs faster, still wrestling with ourselves and allowing the foolishness to evade our sense of know better, but, most of the time, we get to the end again. The hardest break up to fathom though is breaking up with yourself. I've seen it countless times as a clinician and experienced it repeatedly from my teens through my thirties. Each new relationship with myself triggered by a self-manifesto that I was ready for a change, cued a sense of doubt that this time would be different, and thus, my new unhealthy relationship habits with myself were born. If you've ever wondered, let me confirm, the power of the habit cycle is very real.

Becoming an entrepreneur was a new kind of trigger for me. It cued a switch that I didn't know existed, one that lit up insecurities and put a spotlight on my 9-year old inner child. Walking into rooms full of older white men in black or blue suits, who looked at me with confusion when I'd approach and introduce myself, started to take its toll on me. Remember, I was a social worker, trauma specialist, and expert in behavioral health before I made my leap into the world of a hunter who also gathers. People were referred to me, and I referred out to others, I never had to go and create cold connections that I directly benefited from. I was like a cute bunny rabbit prancing around the networking woods in front of hungry wolves. Most of the men and many of the women that I'd meet in the first few years of my entrepreneurship venture hid their agendas as they pretended to want to partner with me while bleeding my pockets. It wasn't always money that they'd want. Though many of them tried to convince me of why I needed their services directly, most wanted to use my ethnicity, race, and gender to get close to their target market of women, especially other black women.

My need to be validated would tether me to some of these relationships, regardless of how clear the red flags would stand out and wave at me. Completely out of balance and not admitting the truth of what I wanted, my boundaries were low or non-existence. I overextended myself, showed up early to every meeting, offering to help prepare, taking up leadership roles on countless committees, and giving away valuable strategy for the price of a gluten-free salad. My calendar was overflowing with appointments, and I was always busy as a bee. I'd once again justified the relationship I had with myself, the one that allowed people, places, and things to distract me, by declassifying all the negative behaviors and actions as not so terrible. When I'd get frustrated with myself, I'd say things like, "at least I'm not comparing myself or trying to hold anyone else back from growing like so and so tried with me last year…" Defaulting to the abandoned child who's parents both chose drugs to medicate their pain and fill the void left by their countless stacked traumas, I started to believe that I was unworthy again.

It wasn't until after nearly 4-years into running my company, after a fight with my body and eventual auto-immune diagnosis, post losing over $100,000 in the business, and racking up triple that amount in medical bills that I heard the alarm blare so loud it gave me pause. There was an urgency in this sound; the pitch was deafening and vibrated like never before. The sound screeched over top of Dean's attempts to tell me he felt trapped in a loop inside our marriage, strangling his ability to see himself or his goals. Over the last few years, we'd tried, done well for a while, failed, and tried again to reignite the passion in our marriage. My self-doubt toppled with him, treating me like fragile glass because of my medical condition, mixed with his depression, anxiety, and increased agoraphobic symptoms, smothered out our attempts. Our kids were getting older, their clothes were becoming more expensive, and I was falling deep into the dark cave of a scarcity mindset. Holding on to my faith with a whisper and a prayer, the alarms to break up with myself were blaring.

At this point, we'd incurred quite a heavy financial debt from the snowball of medical bills and previous business bills from my first leap into entrepreneurship wearing a baggy small business owner size vest in my misguided attempt to run a staffing agency. Quick to go into survival mode, I went harder and jam-packed my networking calendar. I made it my business to be in the rooms where my potential clients and partners spent time. That meant attending evening dinners, golf networking events (I don't play golf), weekend brunches, 7 a.m. breakfast meetings, and at least 5-7 one-to-one coffee connection meetings a day. My network widened, and so did my territory. What began as just a few trips to New York once a month expanded to gaining clients from California, Washington, South Africa, Paris and beyond. Of course, some of those client relationships were strictly over video conference strategy sessions; many weren't.

I'd gotten pretty good at recognizing the wolves and filtering who I'd let in or near my network, but I hadn't mastered my need to please. Proud of myself for cutting loose the two or three spiritual and physical energy zappers who hid their envy behind a handshake of friendship, there were still a few leaky holes in my armor, leeches who called themselves friend, some even sister, masked those holes a few months longer than I'd preferred. I couldn't always see them, but I'd feel them. Zapping my energy with "nice" smiles, familiar conversations over wine where they'd informally ask for my professional guidance, telling me how invaluable I was but never offering to invest in any of those programs my company offered.

The wackiest moment repeatedly occurred, like a lesson you refuse to receive. There was one leach who I now see that I allowed to stay on me because there was a bit of comfort in her presence. She showed me time and time again that she didn't value friendship or people for that matter. She'd talk to me about her other friends hypocritically, saying they were beneath her, she was over them, but then hug them with wide arms and full smiles when they were in each other's company. I knew enough to know a dog that brings a bone takes one back, and anything she'd be willing to say about her childhood friends or strategic business partners, she wouldn't hesitate to say about me. And still, I kept her in my inner circle.

What she offered me was the opportunity to fix. I justified her behaviors and reasoned that she didn't know how to trust or be a friend, and I could show her by just being vulnerable and transparent, which she'd already stated she wasn't used to. More than a half dozen times, she'd refer a client to me with a negative disclaimer about their character and/or financial fit, with a caveat that I would be best to help them. It was quite hilarious considering my expertise and investment was higher than hers, but guess what? I'd take their call and provide a free consultation session with them as a favor to her anyway. She'd look like the helping hero, and I'd get to help. The cycle was sickening!

What happens in your personal life, the aggregate of impact from the big and dozens of little stacked traumas, unrelieved stressors, and chisels through your confidence undoubtedly show up in your efficiency and performance at work. There was a mirroring effect reflected in the type of clients and strategic partnerships I'd attract in business. Just as the leaches would zap my energy and pull on my unhealed inner child heartstrings, so would others. It would be years before I'd finally stop attracting a plethora of clients that would show up glammed up, sharing tales of their jet-set life, while simultaneously whispering that they couldn't afford to invest in themselves. The reality was, they were mirrors of me. From the outside, being married to my high school sweetheart, had two kids and a puggle, corner house with a white picket fence, and a tight spiritual circle with in-laws that I loved looked like Oscar winning Pixar film in the making. In reality, we were shattering from the inside out and our life was an image reel where only the best highlights were shown in public. My friendships were *situationships*, seasonal relationships that were passed their expiration date and molding my soul.

## A New Necessary Divorce

It wouldn't be until my son's high school graduation that I would decide to do more than just break up with this toxic version of myself. I had to leave zero room for a make-up period, so I filed for a very necessary divorce— from me. Leading up to my son's graduation, I had a packed schedule with only one workday greyed out for non-core-money many activities, a day for a center city graduation, and celebratory dinner with family. By this time, I was inflexible. As I shared earlier, my calendar was my second bible and as a loyalist, it would take a near-death emergency for me to cancel or reschedule anything or anyone once I had it penned in ink. Just like I have a physical, page-flipping bible and the digital app, before you ask, I do still carry a paperback planner in addition to my Gmail calendar! I think we've already established I exist along the control freak side of the continuum.

So, when my son's high school noted a change in the graduation date about a month prior to the ceremony, I was faced with what would become my last regret. The new proposed date conflicted with an out of town conference I was scheduled to attend with my social selling mentor and friend who was also the keynote for the event. I knew she would tell me to skip the conference and go to my son's graduation, so I didn't tell her about the conflict. She had no idea how unhealthy my addiction to survival mode had become, how high the internal toxic levels were in my relationship to myself, nor how overwhelmed I felt at the thought of missing a key relationship-building opportunity with ideal clients. Anchored by mental tapes of scarcity playing on a loop, all I kept hearing was the bible verse, "a man who does not work does not eat." - 2 Thessalonians chapter 3:10 KJV. In hindsight, I took that verse completely out of context and conveniently applied it as salve over the wound of my heart from the decision I'd made. In true bad habit repetitious fashion, I'd convinced myself that we needed to give him all the chances we could at making a successful transition into adulthood. With college just a few months away for him and around the corner for his sister, a freshman in high school at the time, I couldn't afford to miss a networking conference. Instead, I arranged for his godmother to go in my stead to celebrate what I should've witnessed.

That was the last straw. When I called and spoke to my son after graduation, I could hear between his phrases of pacification, ensuring me that it was okay, he understood that I had to work, that he was disappointed. I hadn't been a drug addict or alcoholic as my parents had been, but here I was, once again, choosing my addiction to the stress created by inner child demand to be 75% different, over my children. Like someone addicted to an external substance, I had a rush of adrenaline and a double shot of dopamine every time I was in a hectic situation. The rush of dopamine to my brain's reward center increased at least three-fold if that stress was rooted in limiting beliefs about what would or wouldn't happen if I didn't save or fix something or someone.

Years of therapy to deal with my trauma, the countless coaching programs I'd invested in to grow my business, and the multitude of degrees and certifications that sat on the shelves of my home office, and not one of those things helped me understand that I was an addict. My drug of choice, stress-induced from barely surviving. Why? Because I became a master of compartmentalizing and hiding behind the makeup of my ambition & giving. Not too different from a battered woman, who's brilliant enough to cover up the shame of the morning's tussle with a highly matched skin foundation and eyeshadow, I masked the scars and bruises left from the constant stress of survival mode with high performance, ambitious completion of near-impossible projects, and generous giving. By never painting the *whole picture* for any one advisor, coach, therapist or the like, they could only see the pieces I'd allow them to see, blinded to my reality. As I tended to present as someone well put together, and aware, I could easily stress the one area of my life I declared as the issue, and de-emphasize the need for them to aide me with discovering or filling holes in my whole life.

I was in a really bad relationship. Constantly separating issues, problems, behaviors, and traumas from each other so they wouldn't overwhelm me and force a decision I didn't trust I was strong enough to handle. I needed more than therapy. I needed to stop living for other people and start living for myself. But I had to want me more than I wanted to fix other people. My brilliance could no longer cover up the pain I was in every day, bound and unbalanced. I had to want something more than just barely surviving. My past traumas, current addiction, and toxic relationship with myself had pushed me into a corner and landed me in front of a mirror I couldn't look away from. It was time for something new, a new and very necessary divorce.

The next major paradigm shift of my life occurred after I divorced myself that year. I loosened up, got a bit more spontaneous, even started watching television again. Outside of passing through the living room as my history-buff husband would absorb countless documentaries, history channel dramedies and everything sports, I hadn't turned on a T.V since I started my doctorate program in 2008. My daughter introduced me to a show called Once Upon A Time that was very teen fantasy, and it perked up my curiosity. We'd watch it together as a form of mommy-daughter time and discuss the corny or silly points about the storyline. When she faded interest in that series, we moved to Vampire Diaries and The Originals on Netflix. A definite must-see by the way. It was a weird and vibrant feeling to carve out time in front of the boob tube.

I didn't grow up watching a lot of television, so it wasn't really a big deal for me not to watch it as an adult. For my kids, it mattered for me to be able to share thoughts about storylines and be a little more modern, so for their sake, it was worth trying. Little did I know, I'd like it too. Over time I'd find myself giggling, then full-on laughing with Dean over stand-up comedy shows and family-oriented series like Blackish and Fresh Off the Boat on Hulu. Divorce had given me the freedom to be comfortable in my own skin, to live a little more and let go of the burden I carried trying to control everything. Learning to laugh again, to enjoy time and space, opened me up to more than just time with family, I was able to deepen connections with everyone who mattered, starting with myself.

# Reflect & Celebrate
## *Lessons Learned*

We've all heard countless times that our greatest opportunities live on the other side of our comfort zones. But no one shares that what we will be exposed to when we get to the other side will cause us to navigate through several world altering paradigm shifts. Each shift is required, shattering larger amounts of calcified chaos and confusion built from our stress, stacked traumas, and insecurities.

Our purpose, the very thing we seek to find, that we pay other people to give us clarity around, is hidden underneath the fossilized pain. The shifts that chisel, break, and shake our comfortable worlds is extremely uncomfortable, awkward (and) necessary.

Resisting it doesn't stop it from occurring, but it does slow us down from receiving the opportunity to participate in what's possible on the other side of ourselves.

Choose to experience it, and the reward is great (and) deep. Choose to resist and stay stuck in survival mode, exhausted from battling yourself.

Either way, a choice is required.

# Section V:
# Create Your Joy

If we allow ourselves to move beyond surviving and push beyond balance, we will enter an immeasurable unconquerable space. This renewed space of possibilities is where we go deeper, further into the more we've been searching for. This space is where we amplify intimacy and thrive in all areas of our work, life, and love. It is crucial that in this hour of our lives, we do not seek to find our joy; instead, we create.

# Moving Beyond Balance

## 11

There is so much more to do in your life after you've figured out exactly what you're meant to do with it. I spent over two decades trying to find my purpose on this planet. Quietly shed pounds of tears and disrupted my husband with a restless twist and turns amidst countless sleepless nights. For the greater portion of my professional career, I developed my skills, talents and sharpened my gifts by solving problems and designing solutions for people my inner superwoman wished I could save. So many good things were produced with the best intentions; sadly, most of them were distractions that pulled me away from the truth of what I really wanted in life. I believe in destiny, a knowing that there is something specific that I must accomplish, perhaps one person that I must activate before my head is laid to rest. With that, I understand that the detours I took along my journey, haven't changed the trajectory of my destination, but perhaps a few of them deferred it a bit. Not all, but some of those detours could've been avoided, had I slowed down and listened to the lesson that came before it.

Eventually, I moved into a space where creating balance wasn't just a show of possibility or a point to prove. When I finally opened myself up to the idea that transparent alignment would rid me of my addiction and cement my work/life balance, I was like a new mom, overprotective of her baby. Everywhere I turned, there were gurus, influencers, and celebrities discrediting the phrase "work/life balance." Naysayers that leveraged semantics and switch out the original term for complimentary synonyms like integration, enrichment, or harmony aided me in sweeping out the residue leftover from my old story. It took a bit, but I went from fierce protection and eloquently assertive debates over the assertion that work/life balance was achievable, to finally appreciating that there was no need to yell and point out what is undeniable. My life is a testament, as are the lives of so many men and women I've worked with over the years. If you believe that you can create your own reality, then you must also believe you can have balance, if you're willing to create that too.

Letting go of unhealthy relationships and forgiving myself allowed me to see the cliff notes guide to growing through to get to my next step. Accepting the brash chisel of lessons that repeated until I passed the test prepared before me, propelled me towards the paradigm filled with shifts that would shake me free from the expectations that bound my brilliance to that hurt little girl holding on to early scripts as her blueprint. I'd receive the blessing of wisdom from the creator of the universe, who gave me peace and knowledge that as awesome as I am, I can create, but I'm not in control. Trusting that there is something bigger than me, pulling me forth, yet empowering me to create the beauty along the road that I journey towards my destiny is in itself fulfilling.

As one of my incredible coaches pointed out, I'd uncovered my Ikigai, Japanese, for a reason for being. Philanthropy, lifestyle flexibility, and purposeful positioning were personal motivations that now underline my personal development company for women and men across the world. With confidence and glee, I permitted myself to incorporate unapologetic boundaries around my faith, perspectives, personal expectations, energy capacity, and healthy habits. One would think that with all this revelation and inspired action, I would sit myself down somewhere and relish in gratitude at this point, right?

I did just that. I'd received so many spiritual downloads over the next few years, and with each one, I tried to infuse that new level of awareness into my work and my life. From the outside, our company's program offerings, collateral, and tagline evolved, reflecting the internal shifts it's CEO was experiencing. No matter what the new branding or marketing campaign looked like, the cornerstone of the work was always focused on the growth and development of the person *inside* the professional. Regardless of the niched name I'd choose from year to year or program to program, that foundation was laid in my vision from so many years ago and purposed just for me.

## Deeper, Further, More...

Like all good things that come to an end, so did my long, non-linear journey to discover my purpose. It was found, and with it, a new doorway was revealed. God began to show me the world with new eyes, heightened intuition, enhanced empathic abilities. My normal survival addicted, boisterous, negligently non-observant, people-pleasing, validation seeking narrative was not allowed here. If I tried to flip back to those comfortable pages filled with the earlier scripts that dictated unfruitful behavior, the air around me thickened, and bated breath would bring me to my knees. Praying mercy on my soul and praising God for soundness of mind and release from old patterns, I could stand again, and revel in a level of consciousness that felt dreamy, ethereal, safe.

Shaking the shame, sharing my testimonies, and admitting my truth authorized a push, moving me beyond balance. No longer addicted to the stress induced by surviving, I have clearance to attract and maintain healthy relationships and deepen connections with every human I choose to accept in my life. There will always be change agents, both attracted and appointed, to show me a new wedge of space for me to create in. Still, I choose who I consent to strengthen a bond with. Reignited, reconnected, and amplified, with more quality than the quantity of time spent, all of my current relationships have been successfully formulated with honest communication and honored agreements. My soul's half, Dean, my children, grandchildren, blood, and beyond blood family members now have a part of my heart that was previously hardened. Embracing my regal responsibility as a daughter to the King of Kings, I operate with the ability to lift others with the tools I've had the privilege to receive. My life is filled with deep hugs, laughter, dancing, singing as my vocally trained teen squirms at the sound, and living life instead of over-scheduling activities.

With kindness and unapologetically gentle honesty, I hire passionate initiative takers who value my evolving servant leadership style and can handle what I've been told is a file cabinet size brain. Having the audacity to create my own joy means I get to selflessly serve at the highest level and initiate a movement comprised of other selfish women who dare to get what they want. I now want to take care of myself before anyone else. I can nourish others from the lessons learned, curated in the vessel that was crafted from the pain that I alone endured. I have the honor of attracting more opportunities that I can say no to, without explanation or apology. My time on this earth is precious, so my victory to overcome the early scripts imprinted on my life is not by luck or chance; it is intentional. I'm all in. Embracing the change, I no longer resist but invite to a seat the table, celebrating the small wins and taking bigger calculated leaps are tenants for my blueprint for success. For that reason, I choose to change the conversation and redefine what it means to get selfish and give myself all the permission necessary to live a life of (and) not or....

# ABOUT THE AUTHOR

Naketa R. Thigpen, LCSW, regarded as the #1 Balance & Relationship Advisor in the World, is the President & CEO of ThigPro Balance and Relationship Management Institute, a global personal development company head-quartered in Philadelphia, PA that's revivifying the industry.

A Transformative Empowerment Speaker in demand to lead main stage keynotes, create custom business accelerators, coaching circles, and live retreats, Naketa, and her team set out every day to inspire, equip and empower the willing ambitious women (and a few brave men) who are ready to change the narrative to amplify intimacy and have more freedom, flexibility, and confidence to thrive in work/life (and love). **Ultimately**, helping you to create your balance (and) create your joy.

Ignited to Activate others, Naketa's authored several books and workbooks with her latest scribe being her personal transformation book *Selfish: Permission to Pause, Live, Love & Laugh Your Way to Joy*. Featured on the Lifestyle Channel, International Radio shows and broadcast, recipient of the NAACP award as one of 101

Top Influencers in Philadelphia and NAPW Women of Excellence, Naketa has set her daily intention to empower and motivate the willing and shares lessons, tools and techniques through her weekly Balance Boldly Podcast, Let's Talk Intimacy Livestream and upcoming internet show, The Intimacy Advantage in Business.

While prioritizing her first ministry to her family, as a wife, mother, and newly appointed charge as *g-bunny* (grandmother), Naketa has earned several post-graduate certifications, and is active in the community as a mental health & wellbeing advocate, passionate champion for healthy relationships, and marketplace-minister.

Connect with Naketa @AskNaketa on Twitter and Instagram.
For more information, please visit www.thigpro.com or email at admin@thigpro.com

Subscribe to the Balance Boldly Podcast for Ambitious Women In Business (and a few brave men) on your favorite podcast app https://link.chtbl.com/balanceboldly

Made in the USA
Middletown, DE
14 June 2020